Episcopal Questions, Episcopal Answers

Exploring Christian Faith

IAN S. MARKHAM & C. K. ROBERTSON

Morehouse Publishing
NEW YORK · HARRISBURG · DENVER

Morehouse Publishing, 4785 Linglestown Road, Suite 101, Harrisburg, PA 17112

Morehouse Publishing, 19 East 34th Street, New York, NY 10016

Morehouse Publishing is an imprint of Church Publishing Incorporated.
www.churchpublishing.org

Cover design by Laurie Klein Westhafer
Typeset by Rose Design

Library of Congress Cataloging-in-Publication Data

Markham, Ian S.
 Episcopal questions, Episcopal answers : exploring Christian faith / Ian Markham and C. K. Robertson.
    pages cm.
Includes bibliographical references.
 ISBN 978-0-8192-2309-8 (pbk.)—ISBN 978-0-8192-2914-4 (ebook) 1. Episcopal Church—Doctrines—Miscellanea. I. Title.
BX5930.3.M37 2014
283'.73—dc23
                              2013042418

Printed in the United States of America

We dedicate this book to our respective children—
Luke Markham and David, Jonathan, and Abby Robertson—
here is hoping that you find the Episcopal Church provides
some of the answers to those difficult life questions you will face

Contents

Section Two:
Ethics / 42

Section Three:
Church Architecture and Vestments / 53

Section Four:
Scripture / 56

SECTION FIVE:
SACRAMENTS / 64

SECTION SIX:
BOOK OF COMMON PRAYER / 72

SECTION SEVEN:
THE CHURCH / 83

SECTION EIGHT:
ANGLICAN COMMUNION / 93

SECTION NINE:
AND FINALLY . . . / 101

Acknowledgments

We are grateful to Davis Perkins for the invitation to write this book. We are grateful to our respective colleagues who understand how important writing is for us—to Presiding Bishop Katharine Jefferts Schori and to the Board and Senior Team of Virginia Theological Seminary.

We are especially grateful to colleagues who help make our days manageable: Katherine Malloy and Ednice Baerga.

As the manuscript was near completion, we are grateful to the Rev. Dr. Barney Hawkins, the Rev. Dr. James Farwell, and the Rev. Gray Magganio. They gathered for an evening and shared their questions and thoughtful comments on the manuscript. We are also grateful to Ms. Shannon Preston and Ms. Isabella Blanchard who worked hard to finalize the manuscript for the publishers.

Finally, we are grateful to our respective wives—Lesley and Debbie—who understand our preoccupation with writing and tolerate our absence as we finish a section. And we are two fathers who pray often for our children: so we offer this little book to them.

Ian Markham and Charles Robertson

We want you to enjoy thinking about the questions and musings on the answers. The following introduction gives you a sense of the history of the Episcopal Church, but if you want to go straight to the Q&A, skip this introduction and come back later.

Introduction

"What do Episcopalians believe about . . . ?" Despite the name of this book, this seemingly clear-cut question is not necessarily an easy one to answer, at least on one level. Today's Episcopal Church is anything but homogeneous. We have congregations in every state of the Union, as well as in Puerto Rico and the Virgin Islands, Haiti and the Dominican Republic, Honduras and Venezuela, Colombia and Ecuador, Micronesia and Taiwan, and a convocation of churches in Europe. English, Spanish, French, and several other languages can be heard every week in our churches. In our affiliations and in our politics, in our backgrounds and in our vocations, we cover the full range of the continuum.

And yet at the same time, with all our diversity we are first and foremost a people of common prayer. Together we share a common heritage, "one Lord, one faith, one baptism." Each time we gather we profess, "We believe in one God." While never losing sight of the differences that make us many, the pages that follow reflect those commonalities that make us one—that make us not simply Christians, but Episcopal Christians. As such, it is hoped that these questions and answers will prove helpful for long-time members and interested seekers alike, as a means of deepening understanding about who we are and what we are about. Before diving in to the Q&A, however, it might be useful to step back a bit, offer some historical context, and consider what is the first question of the book, "Who are we?"

NEW TESTAMENT ROOTS

Our roots extend back a long way. Indeed, one could say that the Episcopal ethos can be found at the very beginning of Christianity, in a place called Antioch. There an "encouraging" newcomer-turned-church-leader named Barnabas and his bold apprentice, Saul of Tarsus, helped form something connected to, but distinct from, the church in Jerusalem. In the latter, Peter and the other apostles preached and healed, but did so always in the shadow of the Jewish temple. Their group, "the Way," as it was known, was an inspiring, Spirit-filled community, but it was still a Jewish sect and its leaders still went daily to the temple where sacrifices were made.

Antioch was something else entirely, where Greeks as well as Jews heard the Good News proclaimed and formed a faith community entirely separate from temple and sacrifices, an intentionally diverse yet unified community. As is clear in the eleventh chapter of Acts, it was in Antioch, not in Jerusalem, that the disciples were first called Christians. And it was from Antioch that Barnabas and Saul (now Paul), a new breed of apostolic missionaries, were sent forth to plant communities of faith, love, and hope wherever they went. Again, these churches would be marked by diversity as well as unity: "There is neither Jew nor Greek, slave nor free, male nor female, but all are one in Christ." It was rarely an easy task, for diversity is a nice word to say but a hard reality to appreciate. In places like Corinth, for example, the wealthier church members did not want to wait for those field workers and others on the lower socioeconomic level before having their communal meal. The battle over recognizing the uncircumcised may now seem quaint, but then was quite grim.

Still, often despite its own infighting, the movement flourished. And what began there in one small part of the Mediterranean region soon spread throughout the Roman Empire, eventually reaching even the British Isles. Tradition has it that no less a figure than Joseph of Arimathea, the follower of Jesus who donated his own tomb for the Crucified One's burial, traveled to those Isles and planted the gospel, where it took root and grew. Legends surround the misty origins, but certainly by the time of the Council of Nicaea in 325, there were Christians in Britain. Representatives from there attended that council from which emerged the Nicene Creed that is still proclaimed week after week in our churches.

THE CHURCH IN ENGLAND

Over two hundred and fifty years later, those same isles witnessed the arrival of a somewhat reluctant missionary-monk from Rome named Augustine, sent by Pope Gregory, called "the Great." This monk was to bring the faith to the land of the Anglos, or "angels" as Gregory called them. Augustine set up his base in the southeastern region known as Kent, where Aethelbert was king, for there the faith was already in existence, the queen herself being a believer. But the faith he encountered there looked and felt different than that which was familiar to Augustine. It was a Celtic form of Christianity, not Roman. Augustine wrote to Gregory, sharing his concerns, asking how he might show those Celtic Christians the error of their ways and help them to be more Roman. Gregory's reply evidences great wisdom as well as patience, urging Augustine to take the best of what he found, along with the best of what he brought with him, and worry less about the rest. It was a response worthy of Barnabas the Encourager. Eventually, Roman ways would indeed win out, as prescribed at a synod or meeting in a northeastern town called Whitby, but Celtic ways and Celtic leaders would continue to shape Christianity in the Isles as it developed into something connected to, but somehow distinct from, the religious establishment in continental Europe.

Fast-forward several centuries to Tudor England, to the days of Henry VIII. Though perhaps most famous for his ill-fated wives, Henry originally fancied himself something of a theologian. He is said, in fact, to have authored *In Defense of the Seven Sacraments*, a treatise attacking the Protestant reformer Martin Luther, for which the pope awarded the English monarch the title "Defender of the Faith" (a designation eventually bequeathed by Parliament to Henry's heirs). The king's break with Rome is at least ostensibly well known, though the situational complexities that led to the break are often ignored. It has been far easier for many to focus solely on Henry's anger against the pope for refusing him the annulment he sought in order to pursue a second marriage. There were, however, other factors that led to the break beyond the king's need for an heir and his romance with Anne Boleyn. Increasing frustration had been developing for some time against perceived clerical abuses and financial corruption, including involuntary revenue assessments that put English money into Rome's coffers without consultation. This undisputed foreign authority was something with which Henry would not abide.

In an amazingly short time, the king severed the ties that for centuries had bound his realm to the pope and Roman Christianity. He closed down many monasteries, allowed formerly celibate priests to get married and have children, and ordered all worship to be in English rather than Latin. No longer would his church be Roman Catholic.

Neither, however, would it be Protestant. The services were now in the language of the people, but they were still catholic in form and feel. Monasteries were dissolved, but the monastic rhythm of prayer left an indelible mark on what emerged. Henry bequeathed to his realm something familiar but new. The church in England was evolving into the Church of England.

THE ENGLISH REFORMATION

At the heart of this evolution was the Book of Common Prayer. The original edition was published in 1549, two years after Henry's death and his son Edward's ascent to the throne. It was a remarkable work created by Thomas Cranmer, Henry's hand-selected archbishop of Canterbury, chief prelate in the English church. It was Cranmer who, as a university scholar, first attracted Henry's attention when he offered a theological and political solution to the king's "privy matter," arguing that Henry did not need papal permission to divorce his first wife, Catherine of Aragon. What was needed, Cranmer asserted, was discussion with England's own theologians who not only were learned but also sensitive to the needs of their own social and political milieu. Traditions from long ago and far away were important, acknowledged the archbishop, but so were local context and reason.

Thus, while others in continental Europe were making sweeping changes to Christian worship and organization, the reformation that spread across England's shores was more subtle . . . but no less revolutionary. The monarch, not the pope, was now the head—later the "supreme governor"—of the Church. Clergy were allowed to marry and have children. Monies no longer went to Rome. Everything was open to revision, as the opening words of Archbishop Cranmer's preface in the first Prayer Book make clear: "There was never any thing by the wit of man so well conceived, or so surely established, which (in continuance of time) hath not been corrupted."[1] It was because things necessarily changed that intentional change was needed.

The most obvious of Cranmer's changes, of course, was that the liturgy prescribed in the Prayer Book was no longer in Latin, long recognized by the religious authorities in Rome as the only appropriate language for worship. Now the liturgies of the Church would be in the

---

1. Book of Common Prayer, 866.

vernacular, in English, a language "understanded by the people." Likewise, the Prayer Book contained virtually everything that was needed by worshippers and worship leaders alike. Between its covers were the forms for Morning and Evening Prayer, the litany, Holy Communion, as well as Baptism, confirmation, marriage, prayers for the sick, and a funeral service. The "propers," the readings assigned for each day were included along with the "collects," the prayers that collected the themes of each day. Thus, while Cranmer retained bishops and priests, he bridged the gap between them and the laity by making sure that they all had access to the same resource in a language understood by all. The Prayer Book was therefore an empowering tool.

It was also a literary masterpiece. Along with Shakespeare's works and the King James Bible, the Book of Common Prayer helped reinvent the English language, giving it both a breadth and a profound depth that had not previously been uncovered. It was not simply the vocabulary, but the cadence and rhythm of the writing that made it both exquisite and memorable. Grounded in Holy Scripture, inheriting forms and structures from Roman and Lutheran liturgies, Cranmer went to a new level altogether in what he produced, encouraging the ordained ministers to be "stirred up to godliness themselves" and the lay people to be "more inflamed with the love of true religion."

Cranmer also offered a more disciplined and respectful approach to the complexities of the Bible than some of his contemporaries who instead resorted to a kind of proof-texting. The scriptures were like meat to be chewed on, and not the sixteenth-century equivalent of cotton candy to be swallowed whole and found to be without substance. As it says in one of the Prayer Book collects, Christians are called to "read, mark, learn, and inwardly digest"[2] the Scriptures. Even as he joined the continental reformers in their concern for sin and redemption, Cranmer also noted in his collect for Ash Wednesday, the beginning of the penitential season of Lent, God's deep love for humankind, rooted in creation: "Thou hatest nothing that thou hast made, and dost forgive the sins of all them that be penitent."[3]

Even so, Cranmer was not quite satisfied with his first attempt, and so it was only a few years years later that he released what would become the first revision of the Book of Common Prayer. The 1552 edition

---

2. Book of Common Prayer, 236.

3. Book of Common Prayer, 166.

was more Protestant in its tone and feel, something that would have been far too much for Henry's taste. The king, after all, had still been very much a Catholic in his self-understanding. The issue to him was simply one of authority: Who would call the shots in England—king or pope? Cranmer, on the other hand, was far more attracted to the teachings of Luther and the other continental reformers, but he had always remained fiercely loyal to his king. Now, with young but sickly Edward VI on the throne surrounded by Protestant advisors, the archbishop was able to move forward with reforms that would have been impossible under Henry, while always stopping short of the excesses he saw occurring across the English Channel. In his additional reforms—including the publication of English Canon Law and the Forty-Two Articles of Religion (eventually downsized to thirty-nine)—Cranmer always moved in a step-by-step process, seeking continuity when possible and moderate change when needed.

Cranmer's days came to an end after Edward's short reign, when the young king's half-sister Mary came to power. Interestingly, Henry had once sought permission from the pope to divorce Catherine of Aragon because the only surviving child she bore was female, and therefore by tradition was unable to reign as Henry's heir. Yet now it was that same child, Mary, who ascended the throne and returned England to its Roman Catholic roots—by force. Her nickname, "Bloody Mary," was not bestowed on her by accident. Among those slaughtered during her reign was Archbishop Cranmer. An unlikely martyr, the now-aged reformer actually recanted all his theological innovations after being imprisoned and tortured. He was no Martin Luther boldly declaring, "Here I stand, I can do no other!" No, Cranmer signed whatever they put before him, desperate to end the pain. It is, therefore, all the more incredible to witness the end of his story. When brought out before the crowds for his execution at the stake, Cranmer was invited to recant once more for the sake of his own soul and as an example to all the spectators. Instead, he shocked everyone (perhaps himself as well) by recanting his recantation! Cranmer's words have resounded through the years: "And forasmuch as my hand hath offended, writing contrary to my heart, my hand shall first be punished, for when I come to the fire, it shall be first burned." True to his word, when led to the stake, he stretched out his "offending" hand toward the torch. His courage at the end would be Cranmer's great legacy—that, of course, and the Prayer Book that he composed.

THE MIDDLE WAY

The seeds Cranmer had planted began to bear great fruit with the coming of Elizabeth I, daughter of Henry and Anne Boleyn. The well-known golden age that flourished during her reign included a renewed call for religious moderation. By her admission, Elizabeth had no desire to "read into men's souls," but rather allowed for some breadth of thought and personal piety, as long as there was peace in the land and respect for the crown. 1559 witnessed the introduction of a slightly revised version of Cranmer's 1552 Prayer Book, bringing back some elements from the earlier 1549 book that appealed to more liturgically traditional worshippers. Also during Elizabeth's reign arose the theologian Richard Hooker, whose writings on Church "polity" or governance emphasized reason and tolerance alongside Scripture and tradition as crucial to the community of faith in England. His writings countered the extremes of a reactionary Roman Catholicism on the one hand and a radical Puritanism on the other. Indeed, Hooker spoke of the "middle way" that would become the hallmark of Anglicanism, and a natural outgrowth of the ways of Cranmer and, indeed, of both Gregory the Great and Augustine of Canterbury.

The need for a middle way would be evident once again a century later, following the violence of the English Civil War and the return to some sense of normalcy in the land. The result was the 1662 Book of Common Prayer, the preface of which affirms that "it hath been the wisdom of the Church of England, ever since the first compiling of her Public Liturgy, to keep the mean between the two extremes," thereby honoring the "main body and essentials" while allowing for "changes and alterations . . . as seem necessary or expedient."[4]

THE CHURCH IN AMERICA

Such changes and alterations were certainly necessary another century hence as the American Revolution gave birth to a new nation. As the preface to the 1789 American Prayer Book attests, "When in the course of Divine Providence, these American States became independent with respect to civil government, their ecclesiastical independence was necessarily included." Similarities between these words and those of the Declaration of Independence are hardly coincidental, as

---

4. Book of Common Prayer 1662, 7.

the Rev. Dr. William Smith of Maryland, who wrote the preface, was a friend and colleague of Founding Father Benjamin Franklin. While he focused on the new Prayer Book, the Rev. William White, formerly chaplain to the Continental Congress and friend of many renowned personages such as Franklin, John Adams, and Benjamin Rush, turned his attention to the Constitution of the newly independent Church. White, who would go on to be bishop of Pennsylvania and first presiding bishop of the Episcopal Church, had earlier penned an argument for the creation of an independent Church, one that would "contain the constituent principles of the Church of England and yet be independent of foreign jurisdiction of influence."[5]

Here again we see the emphasis on a middle way between breaking completely from the past and being bound by it. As stated in the 1783 document *Declaration of Certain Fundamental Rights and Liberties of the Protestant Episcopal Church of Maryland*, what was sought was only such revision as was needed to reflect "the change of our situation from a daughter to a sister Church." The desire was that, even as the Church became independent, still there would be continuation of the doctrine and worship of the Church of England "as near as may be."[6]

Decision-making in this "Protestant Episcopal Church in the United States of America" would ultimately rest not with a king or queen, or even with an archbishop, but with the General Convention, a legislative body composed of lay leaders as well as bishops and clergy. It was the first General Convention assembled at Christ Church, Philadelphia, on September 27, 1785, that authorized the revision of the Prayer Book and the framing of the Church's Constitution. Although he did not attend that initial national gathering, the Rev. Samuel Seabury had already been consecrated the first bishop in the former colonies some ten months earlier. Having failed to persuade bishops in the Church of England to ordain him, he went to Aberdeen, to the Scottish Episcopal Church, where he was able to find the three bishops required for a valid consecration. William White and two

---

5. William White, *A Case for the Episcopal Churches in the United States Considered* (Philedelphia: David C. Claypoole 1782), preface.

6. William Smith, *Declaration of Certain Fundamental Rights and Liberties of the Protestant Episcopal Church of Maryland* (Annapolis, MD: Diocese of Maryland Convention 1783) as cited in William S. Perry, *Historical Notes and Documents Illustrating the Organization of the Protestant Episcopal Church in the United States of America* (Claremont, NH: Claremont Manufacturing Company, 1874), 22.

other colleagues had better luck a short time later when they went to England and received the laying on of hands there, thus giving the new Church four bishops who could then, in turn, ordain clergy and other bishops. With this "American Succession" of bishops, as with the liturgy of the Prayer Book, there was a desire for continuity in the midst of obvious change.

In the years that followed, although it would never be the largest of the new country's Christian denominations, it would be one of the most influential. Among the Episcopal Church's members have been George Washington, Franklin D. Roosevelt, Gerald Ford, and George H. W. Bush, along with several other presidents—indeed, more than a quarter of all our nation's chief executives, far more than any other religious group. In the earlier years of the nation, this tendency may have been due in large part to the fact that the Episcopal Church was the direct descendent of the Church of England, and in states like New York and Virginia, it had been the state religion. St. John's Episcopal Church, Lafayette Square, just across the park from the White House, is known as the "Church of the Presidents." Starting with James Madison, every president has attended services there at least once, if not many times. Most recently, President Barack Obama went to St. John's on the morning of his second inauguration. A few miles away, on the top of Mount St. Alban's, the highest point in the nation's capital city stands Washington National Cathedral, an Episcopal church that serves as the official seat of both the bishop of Washington and the presiding bishop. Charted by Congress in 1893, the cathedral has long served as the site of funerals and memorial services for presidents, Supreme Court justices, and other national dignitaries, as well as services at times of national celebration or crisis, such as after the tragic events of September 11, 2001. Often called the "spiritual home of the nation," the cathedral welcomes people of all faiths, hosting many interreligious prayer services and dialogues.

CHANGE AND CONTINUITY

Throughout the nineteenth century, the Church wrestled with how to be faithful to what it had inherited in the midst of struggles all around it. African-Americans such as Absalom Jones and James Theodore Holly wrestled with the prejudices of their day and helped take the first steps toward abolition and equality. In 1804 Jones became the first African-American ordained priest. Though he later became part of the nascent Methodist Church, before that he helped open the first black Episcopal church, in the city of Philadelphia, and cofounded the Free African Society, designed to help freed slaves. Later, in the middle of the century, Holly founded the Protestant Episcopal Society for Promoting the Extension of the Church among Colored People, a predecessor to today's Union of Black Episcopalians. He also founded the diocese of Haiti and became its bishop, the first African-American to be ordained to the episcopate. Still, black Episcopalians, like black Americans, faced a difficult road ahead.

And then there were the ongoing challenges to the Church's unity. The creeds we have long proclaimed describe the Church as "one, holy, catholic, and apostolic," but there have always been those who depart from the "one" because they believe it is not "holy" or "apostolic" enough. In sixteenth-century Europe, Anabaptists and other groups went their own way, crying out that Martin Luther and others like him had not gone far enough in their reforms. In seventeenth-century England, Puritans traveled to the New World ostensibly in search of religious freedom, only to shun and even kill those who in some way or another challenged the community's purity. In eighteenth-century America, during the Civil War that engulfed this country, dioceses in the southern states followed their civil authorities and separated from the larger Church, forming the Protestant Episcopal Church in the Confederate States of America. When the war ended, these defecting dioceses were freely received back into the Episcopal Church. But the practice continued: those who disagreed vehemently would at times depart to form something . . . purer, bolder, more faithful.

At the turn of a new century, during the so-called "gilded age," Episcopalians faced a new challenge. "High-church" members published tracts pushing for the use of long-ignored liturgical accouterments such as incense, candles, and more Catholic-style vestments and ways. These "smells and bells" Anglo-Catholics stirred up feelings on all sides. Eventually some, like John Henry Newman, left the Church altogether to go to Rome, even as others from the "low-church" end of the continuum, believing that the Church was giving too much credence to "Romish" ways, broke away to form their own entity, the Reformed Episcopal Church. Other small breakaway groups would follow in the twentieth century, claiming an Anglican identity but separate from what they saw as an errant Church, particularly in areas around worship or engagement with the surrounding culture. Sometimes the two converged, as in the mid-1970s.

As the nation's bicentennial arrived, so much in the country had changed. Two world wars and the arrival of the atomic age had given rise to a new level of general anxiety. Women who followed "Rosie the Riveter" into factories and workplaces when the men had gone to war in the 1940s then found themselves expected to stay at home in the 1950s. The civil rights movement challenged centuries-old assumptions about race relations and the tenet that "all men are created equal." Now women were asking if this applied to them as well. In the previous decades there had been some progress, with women becoming delegates to diocesan conventions and even deputies to the General Convention. They were becoming deacons. But the ages-old barrier was still priestly ordination. In 1975, however, in Philadelphia, eleven female deacons were ordained "irregularly," since it was not yet permitted by the canons, or rules of the Church. This was happening even as yet another Prayer Book revision was occurring, one that took into account the many liturgical discoveries of the last two decades. In the General Conventions of 1976 and 1979, women's ordination was approved and the new Prayer Book was authorized. And, as in years past, this meant that some who could not abide either change broke away from the Church and formed their own group.

Of course, throughout the twentieth century there were momentous changes going on far beyond the United States, changes that would remake the national Church into a multinational, multilingual, multicultural Church. The "Domestic and Foreign Missionary Society of the Protestant Episcopal Church in the United States of America" (the official corporate name of the Church) established missionary congregations and dioceses in various parts of the globe, especially in the Caribbean and in Central and South America. Some of these dioceses eventually came together and formed independent provinces, while maintaining continued close relationships with the Episcopal Church. Mexico, Central America, Brazil, and the Philippines are examples, while Liberia, once part of this Church, joined with its neighboring dioceses in West Africa. Other dioceses—such as Colombia, the Dominican Republic, Ecuador (with two dioceses therein), Haiti (the largest diocese in the Church), Honduras, Micronesia, Puerto Rico, Venezuela—remained as constituent parts of this Church. Spanish and French began to be included alongside English in Church wide meetings, documents, and worship. And as the "foreign" part of the Church grew, the "domestic" parts of the Church likewise found other languages and cultures becoming more and more a part of their own reality.

THE ANGLICAN COMMUNION

Even as our Church grew in its breadth and diversity, so too did the worldwide Anglican family, as those former colonial churches that were outgrowths of the Church of England gradually gained autonomy and, like the British Commonwealth of nations, maintained their connections to the English church and one another by being in communion with the archbishop of Canterbury, who became a living symbol or instrument of unity for what came to be called the Anglican Communion. Now stretched across the globe, these various national and regional churches are both independent and interdependent, and together represent the third largest body of Christians in the world (behind Roman Catholics and the Orthodox). And in recent years, Anglicans in general and the Episcopal Church in particular have delineated Five Marks of Mission to express our purpose and goals. They are: (1) to proclaim the Good News of the kingdom of God, (2) to teach, baptize, and nurture new believers, (3) to respond to human need by loving service, (4) to seek to transform unjust structures of society, and (5) to strive to safeguard the integrity of creation and sustain and renew the life of the earth. These are our marching orders! All the other Marks of Mission are summarized by the first, the proclamation of the Good News. As St. Francis of Assisi once said, "Preach the Gospel at all times; if necessary, use words." As Episcopalians, as part of local congregations and a global communion, we can change our own part of the world by taking seriously the Marks of Mission in our lives, individually and corporately.

ONWARD!

So what do Episcopalians believe about . . . ? As we've seen in this brief introduction, with a heritage as rich and diverse and multilayered as ours, we can be sure that it won't be easy to pin us down on, well, just about anything. However, as has also been evident in this trip through the years, we have seen that, truly, the more things change, the more that the key things, the things that really matter to us, do stay the same. As we said over a century ago in the so-called Chicago-Lambeth Quadrilateral, we remain now as then grounded in the Scriptures, the creeds, the sacraments, and the Historic Episcopate (the line of bishops in succession). However much we may differ in any number of ways, we are still a people on a journey together in Christ, a people with a remarkable heritage and a glorious hope, a people of common prayer. So whether you are a lifelong member of this Church or a curious visitor wanting to learn more, flip through the pages that follow and find out who we are and what we're about. And if our answers here lead to even more questions, then come on down to your local congregation and bring your own questions with you. Dare to join in the conversation. You'll be glad that you did. Come and see, come and experience the ongoing adventure with us.

We are Episcopalians . . . and we welcome you!

Episcopal Beliefs

Is there any evidence that God exists?

In brief the answer is yes. Anglicans tend to be inclined to the view that there are several arguments that suggest the existence of God. Generally Anglican theologians, such as Keith Ward and Eric Mascall, are sympathetic to the project known as "natural theology." Natural theology is the attempt to show that there is in nature and our experience good evidence that God exists. Indeed, the great Roman Catholic theologian Thomas Aquinas (1274) insisted that human reason, without the help of the Bible, was able to establish three truths—namely, the existence of God, the nature of God, and the immortality of the soul.

Although Anglican theologians would not want to overstate the power of these arguments, they are sympathetic to the suggestion that one's view of the world is incomplete unless one affirms the reality of God. Some have talked about pointers to God's existence. These pointers include the big metaphysical questions (e.g., why does anything exist?) as well as the mysteries of experience (what is the source of our moral instincts?).

On the big metaphysical questions, probably the one which is most striking is the emerging mystery around the remarkable improbable mathematics of our existence. This is known as the "anthropic principle." Cosmologists are now in agreement that it is remarkable that this universe is a life-producing universe. To take one illustration, at the Big Bang the relationship between the force of gravity and the expansive force had to be exactly right. If the force of gravity was too strong, then the universe would collapse into itself; if the expansive force was too great, then the universe would just dissipate into a mass of gases and stars and planets that would not have formed. The universe ended up being just right; and the odds of this occurring are the equivalent of taking a gun and hitting a target on the other side of the universe. This is just one of many such remarkable instances. The universe looks as if life was intended. This doesn't surprise Episcopalians because this is exactly what we believe about the universe.

On the mysteries of experience, many Anglican thinkers have felt that the mystery of our moral sensitivity needed explaining. Our sense of moral obligation is puzzling. When we feel that we really "ought" to do something (for example, visit a relative in hospital), the "ought" feels as if it is an external pressure on our life. Although we might wish to go to the movie theater, we are feeling obligated to do something we would rather not do. How do we explain this basic phenomenon? For Anglican thinkers, the strongest explanation was God, the source of all love and justice, who calls all humanity into a deeper relationship through our commitment to live life appropriately.

There are plenty of other arguments, but these are just two illustrations of why Anglicans believe that there is good evidence that God exists.

Additional question: What do you think is the strongest argument for God's existence? Do you think such an argument is possible or necessary for faith?

What is God like?

There isn't a distinctively Episcopalian answer to this question. This is good; after all, we see ourselves as a tradition that builds on and shares the wisdom of the entire Christian tradition. And our church has advocates reflecting the main options in Christendom generally. The classical answer, with which many Episcopalians would identify and perhaps is the one found most clearly in our liturgy, is that God is Spirit, source of everything that is, who is timeless, omniscient (all knowing), omnipotent (all powerful), and perfect love.

The argument for the classical position is this. Given God is the source of everything that is, God must be different from matter. If God was matter, then the question "who made God?" would have some force. But given that belief in God is a belief in a creator, God must be different from matter. Furthermore this source of everything is perfect, which is the reason why we worship God. If God is perfect, then God cannot be constantly changing. And if God doesn't change, then God must be timeless (i.e., there is no duration at all in the life of God). From this timeless vantage point, God has complete knowledge of past, present, and future. In addition, God is able to do anything that can be done (create, perform miracles, end the universe), yet we know from Scripture that this power is entirely used for the purposes of furthering the ends of love.

Some thinkers in the Episcopal Church have more sympathy with an alternative account, which brings God closer to the physical universe. Some even talk of the world being the "body of God" or of the universe existing within God (much like an embryo grows inside the womb of the mother). With these pictures, we have a God who has a temporal life (so time is part of God—God does one thing after another), who has allowed free creatures to emerge within the universe. These free creatures are invited to be "cocreators" with God of the future. On this view, God is able to predict the future, but cannot see the future (after all, it hasn't yet happened). God is not so much timeless and eternal, but everlasting. And given God has created free creatures, it is possible for humans to behave in a way that surprises God. Advocates of this position believe that it is closer with the picture of God in the Bible.

Both of these pictures share the affirmation that God creates the universe (the first out of nothing, the second forming within God's own life) and that God is calling us into relationship. A key factor is our interpretation of Scripture. For the classical position, this account is grounded in philosophical speculation derived perhaps from the logic of Scripture; for the alternative account, it is inspired from the dynamic and description of exactly how God seems to relate to the people of God in Scripture.

Additional question: Which account of God do you find more attractive?

Can I have doubts and still be an Episcopalian?

Yes. One joy of being in a deeply biblical tradition is that we spend considerable time among the Psalms. A psalm is one of the lessons appointed for every service. In the Psalms, the people of God struggle with their faith. They rage with God; they puzzle; and yes, they doubt (see, for example, Psalm 77). The Psalms are our biblical justification of the legitimacy of doubt.

It is often said that the opposite of faith is not doubt, but certainty. When we think about God, we do so from the vantage point of humans. We are small entities in a vast universe; we are trying to work out what the source and creator of the universe is like. We should approach this project with some humility. Our vantage point does not permit certainty. We are called to think, struggle, and discern the truth about God and God's relations with the world.

Given all this, the Episcopal Church recognizes that we are all on a journey of faith. This journey will have many twists and turns. Sometimes our sense and experience of God will be strong; at other times, God will seem to be further away.

As we will discover when we look at the Episcopal Church's view of baptism, we have in that moment a promise from God that God is always close to us, even when it is difficult to live that reality. We take the view that as our commitment and confidence in God fluctuates the beauty of the gospel is that God is holding us in a loving embrace regardless.

For most clergy in the Episcopal Church, they are accustomed to members who have doubts and questions. Access to the sacraments does not depend on passing a theology exam or explaining precisely and in what way you believe the creeds.

Additional question: Reflect on the moments in your life when God has seemed close to you and those moments when God has seemed further away. Why the difference?

Why does God allow evil and suffering?

Pain and suffering are built into all of nature. First, it is built into the structure of the planet. Periodically, the tectonic plates on the earth's crust shift, creating an earthquake; and hurricanes, floods, and droughts inflict different parts of the globe every year. Second, it is built into the cycle of life. Every living thing dies; and pain and illness are part of the regular processes of nature. Third, it is part of the reality of human coexistence. Humans have an extraordinary capacity to inflict additional pain and hurt on each other. From rape to the holocaust, humans can be extraordinarily cruel to each other.

The reason why evil and suffering are such a major problem for faith is that Christians believe that God is both all powerful and, simultaneously, perfect love. The problem is often stated as a conundrum as follows: if God is all powerful, then God must be able to abolish suffering; if God is perfect love, then God must wish to abolish suffering. But suffering exists, therefore God cannot be both all powerful and all loving. This is the problem of theodicy.

Within the tradition, there are two responses to this. One response speaks primarily to the head; the other response speaks to the heart. The head response starts by recognizing that the purpose of creation is not to build an idyllic setting where all human needs are satisfied, but to provide an environment where we can be formed to discover the centrality of love in our lives. So we are born into families where the cycle of life and death is the pattern and we learn the precious nature of time spent with each other; we are born into communities where we have to learn to cope with adversity and challenges together; and we learn that each of us has the option of hating rather than loving and with hate comes pain and hurt. For God to have this universe that can create love, it needed to be like this one. And love is so high a value, this universe is worth realizing.

The problem with the head answer is that it feels so inadequate in the light of so many tragedies we read about and see on television. So perhaps the heart response is more helpful. The ultimate Christian response to the tragedy of evil and suffering is Good Friday. Christians believe that on the cross was the creator of the universe hanging and dying. The point is simple: whatever reason God had for allowing evil and suffering, Christians believe that God got involved and fully participated in the tragedy and demands of human existence. And Good Friday is not the end; it is followed by Easter Sunday. So we affirm that in the midst of the tragic, there is always hope. There is always resurrection. There is always a way through.

Can I believe in evolution and be an Episcopalian?

Yes. Unlike some other Christian traditions, we have no problem with the modern account of the universe informed by science. We start from the assumption that all truth is part of the truth of God. Therefore any discovery in any field needs to be taken seriously. Given the evidence for the theory of natural selection is very strong (there is no reputable biologist working at a nonsectarian university who does not accept that some form of natural selection over a long period of time is part of our origins), we believe that Christians need to accommodate that truth.

For some Christians, the problem is the relationship of the theory of evolution with the narrative of Scripture. As we will see, Episcopalians also believe in the authority of Scripture. However, we do not accept that our interpretation of the opening chapters of Genesis need involve the rejection of evolution.

The first and second chapters of Genesis are best read as "poetic." They start with the declaration that "in the beginning God created the heavens and the earth" and then each stage of creation is ushered in by God speaking. Naturally, it assumed an ancient cosmological model—one where the sun appears as a lamp in the sky and is not the source of the light. However, the point of the narrative is not the cosmology, but the act of God speaking and God creating.

The point of this majestic narrative is that God is the source of everything that is. In addition, this is a world which God loves and is engaged with us. When we speak, we reveal our thoughts. So by analogy, everything that is comes from the thought of God. In the same way our words show others who we are, so the creation shows us who God is. Now the precise mechanism of creation is not actually described in the narrative. So we believe that God's mechanism of creation is being discovered by modern biologists. God created using the mechanisms of natural selection. This means that Episcopalians are able to affirm the truth of Genesis and at the same time affirm the truths being discovered by modern science.

Additional question: How do you understand Genesis 1?

How do Episcopalians respond to the claim that science has made religion redundant?

Many have heard of Richard Dawkins and his attack on religion. Dawkins believes that science has made the God hypothesis redundant. Needless to say, Episcopalians disagree strongly with this.

Naturally, we recognize that the achievements of science are remarkable. We appreciate the discovery of antibiotics and modern dentistry; we also affirm the many discoveries that science is making about the nature of the universe. We have already seen how some of those discoveries seem to point to faith. The very fact of science is evidence for God. Science assumes the universe is orderly and predictable. Such order requires explanation, which Christians believe takes the form of divine intention and agency. In other words, the world is orderly because God wanted it to be a stable and predictable environment, in which we can move and learn how to relate to each other.

However, our primary response is to suggest that science explains an aspect of reality but not all of reality. The truth about our universe is that it is a spiritually infused reality. We are not simply complex bundles of atoms that emerged from nowhere and ultimately will be made extinct. Instead, we are a result of divine purpose; we are made with the capacity to love and reason; and we are intended to discover love and thereby construct a reality that can endure for eternity.

In the same way that art is not simply paint dots on a painting, but a glimpse into the transcendent; in the same way as great music is not simply the mechanical action of the ear turning sounds into messages for the brain, but an invitation to be lifted out of ourselves; so science is the foundation of a reality that is ultimately spiritual.

Additional question: Reflect on the ways in which you see the spiritual infuse reality.

How do we approach the creeds?

The short answer is this: we approach the creeds prayerfully and as a way of understanding who we are worshipping and not simply how we are worshipping. The creeds are our statement of faith: they are our description of the God who is the source of everything that is.

However, a longer answer needs to explain the complexity of the creeds in the Book of Common Prayer. Embedded in the Book of Common Prayer are two creeds within our liturgy; the first is the Apostles' Creed (found, for example, in the service for Morning Prayer), which is often referred to as the elemental creed; and the second is the Nicene Creed (found in the service for Holy Eucharist). In addition, if you turn to the section of the Prayer Book called "Historical Documents of the Church," then you will find "Definition of the Union of the Divine and Human Natures in the Person of Christ" from the Council of Chalcedon, which met in 451 CE, the Creed of Saint Athanasius, the preface to the First Book of Common Prayer (1549), the Articles of Religion, and the Chicago-Lambeth Quadrilaterial 1886, 1888.

Although some of these documents are not technically creeds, they are texts embedded in our tradition, which we as Episcopalians honor. It is G. K. Chesterton who famously wrote: "Tradition means giving votes to the most obscure of all classes, our ancestors. It is the democracy of the dead."[1] The Episcopal Church respects tradition; we want to honor the hard work of those who came before us and seek to be shaped by it in the present.

The Apostles' Creed is a major part of the daily pattern of Episcopal worship. It is the creed used when a person is baptized into the Church. The Nicene Creed is expected to be said after the preaching of the word at the principle worship service of the week (normally, the Sunday Eucharist). Liturgically, the idea is this. Having read from the Written Word (i.e., the Bible), and having stood for the Eternal Word (i.e., the Gospel of Christ), and having listened to the Proclaimed Word (the preacher), we then know what this God we worship is like. And so we stand and reaffirm our faith in the words of the Nicene Creed.

The actual text of the creed that we say on a Sunday is the result of two different councils of the church. The first is the Council of Nicaea, which met in 325; this was the council that clarified the basics of the Trinity, especially the eternal nature of the Son. The second is the Council of Constantinople, which met in 381. In particular, it was this council that added the fuller statement about the Holy Spirit and added the assertions of belief about the church, baptism, the resurrection of the dead, and eternal life. In addition, the church in the West added the phrase "and the Son." The idea is that the Holy Spirit does not simply proceed from the Father (the source of all divinity), but also from the Son (the revealer and redeemer). This addition to the creed was a key element in the break between the Eastern church and the West.

The shorter creed is the Apostles' Creed. As the name suggests, we find the idea circulating with St. Ambrose in c. 390 CE that the twelve apostles jointly composed the text. For a whole host of reasons, this is unlikely. This particular version goes back the early eighth century and is a development of the even shorter Old Roman Creed.

In the historical documents section, we have the longest creed, which is attributed to St. Athanasius (c. 297–371). Again it is unlikely to actually come from St. Athanasius because some of the language and expressions are much later. The creed has two primary sections: the first on the Trinity, and the second on the Incarnation. It is more

---

1. G. K. Chesterton, *Orthodoxy* (New York: Doubleday, 1990), 48.

controversial because it includes two clauses that explicitly condemn to hell those who do not believe.

All three creeds stress the Trinitarian nature of our faith. It is around this fundamental idea that the vast majority of Episcopalians gather. It is also noteworthy that many issues that currently divide Christians are not mentioned. There is no mention of human sexuality or a certain view of Scripture or even the atonement. Episcopalians appreciate the freedom that the creeds provide to recognize that there will be diverse views over some of these issues in the church. However, the Trinity is considered fundamental.

Additional question: Turn to the "Historical Documents of the Church" section of the Prayer Book. Which documents do you find helpful in understanding your faith?

Why do Episcopalians believe in the Trinity?

Belief in the Trinity is a defining characteristic of all Christians. As we have already noted, there might be moments when an individual Christian struggles with the doctrine, but the faith of the Church remains resolutely Trinitarian.

For some Christians, the doctrine of the Trinity looks like a quaint and puzzling sum—an odd sum, where we try and make one equal three and three equal one. However, the idea of the doctrine is to make sense of our distinctive experience of God in Christ. For Christians believe that in the very life of Jesus, we have encountered the Eternal Word of God made flesh. In other words, if you ask Christians how do you know what God is like? Then the answer is: we know what God is like by looking at the life, death, and resurrection of Jesus of Nazareth. It is in that life that God has spoken uniquely and for all time.

One interesting feature of all religions is that, in the end, any knowledge about God depends on God revealing God to us. So Muslims believe that the very Word of God is the Qur'an; Jews believe that the very Word of God is the Torah; and Christians locate the very Word of God in a life. (Technically, the Christian equivalent to the Qur'an is not the Bible, it is the Eternal Word made flesh. The Bible, as we shall see later, is extremely important as the place where we learn about the Eternal Word made flesh.) Now in both Islam and Judaism, traditions emerge that, quite rightly, insisted that the Word of God cannot just "begin," but must in a very real sense be part of the

Eternity of God. After all, anything that God says—God must have been always saying. So Jews and Muslims started talking about the Torah and the Qur'an existing in eternity past; these texts, which are the Word of God, preexisted creation.

Christians made a similar shift. Jesus—the very Word of God made flesh—was a disclosure of the Eternal Word. Using the image "Father" to describe the source of everything, we used the image "Son" to describe the communicating aspect of God. After all, sons often reveal much about their fathers. The creator aspect of God— the Father—sustains and enables everything to be. The revealing and redeeming aspect of God—the Son—shows us what God is like and makes it possible for us to discover wholeness.

One obvious problem arises: creation and revelation are both past events. Creation is approximately 13.7 billion years ago; and the life of Jesus is approximately 2,000 years ago. So there is a third aspect of God that enables the past action of God to be constantly present to us. This third aspect is the Holy Spirit.

The doctrine emerged out of a careful study of Scripture and from our experience of God. Constantly throughout the Bible, we see these three different aspects of God move and connect and interrelate. So, for example, at the baptism of Jesus (see Matthew 3:13–17), we see Jesus (the Word) being baptized, the Father's divine affirmation of the mission, and the Holy Spirit descending like a dove. It is because of this three-fold movement of God that we are baptized in the name of the "Father and the Son and the Holy Spirit."

One important reason why Christians believe in the Trinity is to protect our belief in monotheism. From a Christian perspective, it sometimes looks like the picture of eternity past in Islam and Judaism is that they have the creator sitting alongside the Qur'an or the Torah; it looks like there are two bits of God. For Christians, we wanted to make sure that both aspects of God are brought together to protect the oneness of God. So we talked about Father and Son being one; and as we started thinking about the continuing work of God, the Holy Spirit became important. All three aspects of God are one.

The doctrine of the Trinity is important because it was the vehicle through which the church justified the worship of Jesus. Although there are groups which deny the Trinity, yet worship Jesus, the church determined that logically we can only worship Jesus provided Jesus is both God and human. It is important because it is the only way we can be confident that Jesus shows who God really is. If Jesus is the Word—the utterance—of God made flesh, then Jesus must be God. It is important because it helps us understand how God in God's complexity relates to the experience of the Church.

Now much of this is technical and, in some respects, difficult theology. There are as we have noted earlier, some Episcopalians who struggle with this or that aspect of Christian doctrine. One joy of being an Episcopalian is that we are confident that God's feelings are not hurt if we have seasons in our lives where we don't get this or that doctrine. However, at the heart of Anglican thought is a commitment to the Triune nature of God.

Additional question: There are lots of images for the Trinity. One flame, three torches; or ice, water and steam are all H_2O are examples. Do you find these helpful?

Is it acceptable for a bishop to question fundamental doctrines like the Virgin Birth?

One of the best known bishops in the Episcopal Church is the Rt. Rev. John Shelby Spong (1931–). And he is very well known as the bishop who questioned fundamental doctrines like the Virgin Birth. He was the bishop of Newark from 1979 to 2001. He was born in Charlotte, North Carolina, and has become the most radical of all the bishops in the Episcopal Church. His books have sold over a million copies.

For Bishop Spong, faith must constantly adapt and change or die. He sees himself as a friend of Christianity who is attempting to make sure that it remains relevant and connected to modern America. He talks about writing for the person "in exile"—the person who finds the traditional approach to the faith difficult to understand or to relate to. As a result, he does has a distinctive approach to doctrine. He thinks the Virgin Birth did not occur; he denies the bodily resurrection of Jesus; he has even gone as far to say that theism "as a way of defining God is dead."[2] This radical exploration of doctrine has run parallel with an equally radical commitment to social justice. He has been a strong advocate for feminism, gay rights, and racial equality.

Bishop Spong is part of a significant trajectory found not simply in the Episcopal Church but also in the Anglican Communion. From

---

2. John Spong, *Why Christianity Must Change or Die* (London: Harper Collins, 1999), 59.

the volume of essays called *Lux Mundi* published in 1889 to Bishop John A. T. Robinson in the 1960s, Bishop Spong is in a long line of leaders who have questioned the fundamentals of the faith. Bishop Spong is an example of how the Episcopal Church is a big tent for a vast range of opinion. We have in our ranks conservative evangelicals (who take a very high view of Scripture) and radical, liberal, progressives (like Bishop Spong) and everyone in between. The assumption the Church makes is that the conversation is as important as the conclusion. Although the Episcopal Church as a whole officially affirms the truth embedded in the creeds, we welcome provocative conversation partners who make us think about our faith. And some Episcopalians enjoy the questions as much as the answers.

Bishop Spong has played an important role in keeping those who have doubts and questions in the Church. The Church needs those who push the doctrinal edges. This is an important role that Bishop Spong has played.

Additional question: Do you have doubts about the Virgin Birth?

What do Episcopalians believe about Jesus?

The heart of the Christian faith is the claim that God was in Christ. We follow the rest of the Christian family in affirming the reality and truth of the Incarnation. The doctrine of the Incarnation has been a central and defining characteristic of Anglican theology. The idea that God got involved, participated fully in human existence and, in so doing, models for us the obligation to get involved has shaped Anglican theology for centuries.

Jesus was a Jew who spent most of his ministry in the regions of Galilee (northern Israel) and Judea (further south). He lived a relatively short life, dying tragically in his early thirties at the hands of the occupying Roman Empire. He attracted around him men and women who recognized in the way he taught and related to people the very presence of God. After his tragic cruxifician, a conviction emerged among his followers that he had been resurrected. And so the Jesus movement started.

This in brief is the remarkable story of Jesus. We can track the details in the Gospels (which focus on the life of Jesus) and in the rest of the New Testament (much of which was written before the Gospels and describe the early Jesus movement). One characteristic that bubbles through the text is the way in which these monotheistic Jews (believers in one God who knew it would be wrong to worship anything except God) were worshipping Jesus.

For the Episcopal Church, Jesus is the primary Word of God. As we shall see later, the Bible is the Word of God because it points to the primary Word, which is Jesus. It is from the Incarnation that we learn what God is like. It is the primary disclosure of the nature of God to humanity.

It was at the Council of Chalcedon in 451 CE that the church tried to make sense of the mystery of the Incarnation. Part of the definition is found in the Book of Common Prayer. It states: "Therefore, following the holy fathers, we all with one accord teach men to acknowledge one and the same Son, our Lord Jesus Christ, at once complete in Godhead and complete in manhood, truly God and truly man, consisting also of a reasonable soul and body; of one substance with the Father as regards his Godhead, and at the same time of one substance with us as regards his manhood; like us in all respects, apart from sin."[3] The key idea here is this: Jesus is both completely God and completely human. We are being invited to affirm a mystery, which is located in a person, not in an abstract thought but an incarnate reality.

Naturally, many people find this idea puzzling. One helpful way to think about the Incarnation is to see how the revealing and redeeming aspect of God (the Son) completely interpenetrates the human Jesus. It is a complete interpenetration, so Jesus is completely God and a real person.

It is because of the doctrine of the Incarnation that in much of our Episcopal liturgy we worship Jesus. We do so within the triune life of God. We see in this person who gave himself constantly for others, the presence of God who constantly gives us life made possible by his sacrifice; we see in this person who never gave up on anyone, the presence of God who never gives up on anyone; we see in this person a call for justice and radical inclusion, the reality of God who calls us to justice and radical inclusion. And we see in the cross, the full embrace and participation of God in the tragic, painful, and suffering sides of life.

Additional question: How do you understand Jesus?

---

3. Book of Common Prayer, 864.

What do Episcopalians believe about the Holy Spirit?

For Christians, the Holy Spirit is promised in John 17. Jesus promises that when his physical presence is no longer with the disciples, the Father will send a Comforter. In the book of Acts, we have the dramatic arrival of the Holy Spirit. The Spirit is the agent that connects the continuing presence of Christ to the church; the Spirit is the means through which the Father continues to act in the world. The Holy Spirit is the aspect of God that connects the reality of God to the life of the church and to the world.

The Holy Spirit is a vitally important aspect of God. It is the aspect that constantly calls us to realize the hope promised in the reign of God (in the kingdom of God). Christians know that we must be constantly frustrated with the way things are. We live in a society where justice is denied and where sin corrupts. It is the work of the Holy Spirit that invites the church to be change agents, both in society and in our individual lives.

Some Episcopalians are "charismatics." They believe that the Holy Spirit promises the church distinctive gifts—the gift of speaking in tongues, of healing, and of prophecy (to pick the most spectacular of the many gifts provided by the Spirit). These gifts are resources that can transform the experience of the individual Christian.

In both the social and the individual aspects, the Holy Spirit is the vehicle of the grace of God that enables us to realize the challenge of holy living. God wants us to make love central in our lives. We have strong propensities to selfishness and egoism; it is the Holy Spirit that seeks to "sanctify us." Sometimes this work of sanctification can be difficult; it can be painful. As we allow the Holy Spirit to work, the Spirit will take our damaging egotistical habits and turn us into agents of love that can participate in the work of God that ushers in the realm of God.

Additional question: In what ways is the Holy Spirit working in your life?

How do Episcopalians decide what is right and true in theology?

It was Richard Hooker (1554–1600) who is given the credit for suggesting that Anglicans want to ensure that we recognize both the importance of Scripture and the authority of tradition. In addition, he wanted us to recognize that we were made in the image of God, which means we have a God-given capacity to reason and think. The combination of Scripture, tradition, and reason makes up the famous three-legged stool of Anglicanism.

It is true that the Anglican tradition sees itself in between Rome (the home of the Roman Catholic Church) and Geneva (the home of the Reformed traditions). With Rome, we recognize the importance of an episcopacy (the bishops) in safeguarding the tradition, which is passed down from generation to generation. With Rome, we recognize the importance of the church councils and the decisions made to shape the basics of the Christian faith. And with Geneva, we recognize the importance of Scripture and how, with the help of the Holy Spirit, the text can come alive to the individual Christian. With Geneva, we recognize the imperative of honoring the ministry of all the baptized and how leadership is the simple privilege of service.

Within this framework, the Episcopal Church sees itself in a quest for the truth. First and most important, we recognize that the definitive disclosure of God is the life, death, and resurrection of Jesus. This is the Eternal Word made flesh. A fundamental test of all theology is this: Is this compatible and grounded in what we learn of God in Christ? Second, we listen with care to the voices from the past—the traditions of the church. And third, we listen with care to what the Holy Spirit might be saying through new and different conversation partners. It was William Sparrow, a nineteenth-century dean of Virginia Theological Seminary, who wrote, "Seek the Truth, come whence it may, cost what it will." It is because all truth is God's truth that we listen with care to the voices emerging from the scientific community, to the voices among the marginalized and ignored, to the voices in contemporary culture, and to the voices in other faith traditions.

The Episcopal Church sees this process as discernment. The control on our theology is always what we learn of God in Christ. And given the only source (much as the noncanonical gospels are fun, they were excluded for a good reason) is Scripture, then Scripture must be central. Under this umbrella, we put our tradition in conversation with the continuing discoveries about the nature of the world emerging from science, the marginalized, and other faith traditions. We are willing to modify our understanding of what God expects of humanity in the light of this process of discernment.

This sometimes means that we come across as a tradition which is not clear about what we believe. For Episcopalians, clarity is not always a virtue. We would prefer to be closer to the truth than unequivocally clear in our error. Part of the beauty of the Episcopal tradition is that we live well with the questions; we live well in the realm in between black and white—in the gray.

Additional question: How do you decide what you think is true in your theology?

Did Jesus rise from the dead?

For Christians, the crucifixion is not the end. Good Friday is when God embraces the tragic; Easter Sunday is when God promises the reality of hope. We all share the belief that the resurrection is true; however, there are different understandings of what exactly the resurrection was. The majority of Episcopalians believes that the tomb was indeed empty. This means that the human body of Jesus was transformed into a spiritual body, which according to St. Paul in the book of Romans is an anticipation of the transformation that all our mortal bodies will undergo. Indeed in Romans 8, Paul implies that this transformation is not simply true of all people, but also true of everything in creation.

The conviction that Christ had risen from the dead became the rallying cry of the early Christian movement. All of those early witnesses to this remarkable message of hope were martyred. It was J. B. Phillips, the translator of the New Testament, who talked about the New Testament having "the ring of truth." There were plenty of spectacular texts, for example, one which had a very precocious child Jesus who caused his friends to wither and die when they upset Jesus. This text, along with others, did not make it into the canon. Instead, we have the restrained set of stories written by a group of writers who were relatively close to the events they were describing. It feels like a text that can be trusted.

Episcopalians enjoy Easter. This is the celebration of the resurrection. The hope of the resurrection is the promise that the injustice and suffering of our present age is not permanent. The hope of a different future is a pressure on us all to start creating that different future now. We are here to anticipate and start to let God realize the hope that God has in store for all of us.

Additional question: In what sense do you think the resurrection hope applies to all of creation?

Did Jesus ascend into heaven?

Forty days after Easter, the church marks Ascension Day. The ascension is described in Scripture as the occasion when the resurrected Jesus is received into heaven (see Mark 16:19–20; Luke 24:50–53; Acts 1:9–11). It is the moment when access to the physical presence of Jesus shifts to the agency of Christ through sacraments and through the church. It marks the moment when the Holy Spirit is the primary vehicle of connection with God in our world.

Episcopalians are the type of folks who are happy to affirm the ascension, but would rather not be questioned too closely as to exactly what happened. The narrative does read as if it is assuming a three-tier universe, with heaven just above the clouds, earth as the habitation of humanity, and hell down below the earth. It was Carl Sagan who reportedly said, "If Jesus ascended physically in the sky, and if he arose as rapidly as the speed of light . . . , he would not yet have reached the edges of our galaxy."[4]

To work out precisely what happened is not necessary. If we updated the cosmology, we might find ourselves imagining a Jesus disappearing into a different dimension or passing through a black hole into heaven. But such speculation ignores the point of the doctrine.

The crucial commitment is that the resurrected presence of Jesus does come to an end. As Jesus enters into a state of divine bliss with the divine (namely heaven), so we are invited to meditate on the promise that our participation in heaven is made possible. In addition, it is in the postascension state, that Christ becomes our mediator, advocate, and intercessor. Finally, the church now comes into its own. The church has work to do: it is primary vehicle of the transformation in the world.

Additional question: How do you understand the Ascension?

Is prayer important?

This is a nice easy question. The answer is quite definitely yes. At the heart of our humanity is the connection with the divine that enables us

---

4. As described by John Shelby Spong, *Rescuing the Bible from Fundamentalism: A Bishop Rethinks the Meaning of Scripture* (San Francisco: HarperOne 1992), 31.

to have our being. Prayer is the act of tapping into that divine presence and thereby enabling us to live life more in accord with the demands of love.

Prayer is an enormous privilege. The honor of communing with the creator of the vast universe is extraordinary. Because of what we learn of God in Jesus, we can be confident that God is deeply interested in the details of our complex and often confusing lives. Indeed Jesus compared us with the commonplace sparrow and explained, "Even the hairs of your head are all counted. So do not be afraid; you are of more value than many sparrows" (Matthew 10:30–31). Prayer is a reflection on the value that God places on us.

Episcopalians are expected to find time every day to read the Bible and pray. In the moments we find to spend with God, we are given the opportunity to encounter the holy and invited to strive with a greater commitment toward love. In addition, we can bring our concerns and worries. We can ask God to surround those we love with God's love and peace.

In addition, our corporate worship (those services that are normally on Sunday) is full of prayer. We participate in worship and praise (where we acknowledge the reality of who God is); we come in confession (to admit those moments when we fail and struggle); and we come with our petitions.

Additional question: Given prayer is such an honor, why do we make it such a low priority in our lives?

Does prayer work?

It is important to remember that the primary purpose of prayer is not necessarily to ask God for things. Instead, the purpose of prayer is to connect with our Creator and allow the spiritual dimension of life to call us into a deeper commitment to love. However, Scripture does make clear that from time to time we will have petitions, which Jesus explains we should share with our heavenly Father (Matthew 7:11).

Now petitionary prayer (prayer with requests for divine action) seems puzzling. What is the point of telling one who is omniscient (i.e., knows everything) our needs? Won't God just do the right thing anyway—regardless of our requests and regardless of the number of people who pray? And why is it that someone can desperately pray for the healing of a loved one and that person still dies?

These are good and important questions. However, notice how many of these questions assume that the universe is an uncomplicated predictable machine into which God occasionally takes action. So yes God is omniscient, but God is also in relationship with us and there is every reason to believe that sometimes, between two equally good options, God takes into account our preferences. And perhaps people praying for each other (another very important biblical obligation) creates a power that God can use.

So perhaps we need to think of both God and the universe in a different way. The Anglican theologian Keith Ward has suggested we need to see the universe as a place that is genuinely open to both human agency and divine agency. Although the universe is predictable in so many ways, we know from the New Physics that God has built in an openness that makes all the difference to the possibility of the exercise of free will and divine agency. Perhaps when we pray, we are creating space for God to act. We are opening up channels—perhaps at the quantum level—for love to act and make a difference.

God works within the structures of creation to do what God can do. God does not constantly override human decision to thwart love (so sometimes people do awful things to one another), but God is constantly working with those who are open to love to do what can be done. When the tragic happens, it is still very difficult and painful.

This is an illustration of an Anglican approach to difficult question. Science comes into conversation with Scripture and a picture of prayer slowly emerges.

Additional question: What do you pray for? And what do you expect God to do?

What is heaven like? Is there any evidence for life after death?

For Christians, the primary reason for believing in life after death is the resurrection of Jesus. Jesus is anticipating the state that we will all enjoy. For many Christian theologians, the idea of the resurrection gives us a good sense of what heaven will look like.

If the resurrection is the model, then it seems that there are both continuities and differences with our lives on earth. The continuities are built on our experiences in our life, which means that in some sense we are recognizable; the differences are that we transcend some of the limitation of time and space and that we are liberated from the inevitable connection in this life with hurt and pain.

To our modern minds, this does sound fantastic. So it is at this point that most preachers reach for the slightly overworked analogy of the caterpillar and butterfly. We can all understand the skeptical caterpillar crawling over the sunflower leaves insisting that all this talk about a beautiful butterfly emerging after the molting (shedding) of the exoskeleton (the skin) is a load of nonsense. But it is true.

In the end, there are two contrasting ways we can see life. The first believes that this life is it—this life is everything that is; the second believes this life is set in the context of a bigger picture—a framework that makes sense of this life. The problem with the first way of looking at life is that it makes this life very puzzling. What is this life for if there is no bigger picture? It is for this reason that most Christian thinkers have insisted that life after death is an important framing for this life.

In addition, it is an important part of our response to the problem of evil and suffering. The problem of evil and suffering was exacerbated in the modern period as we became skeptical about life after death. The tragic is even harder to understand if this life is it. However, if this life is part of a bigger picture, where justice will triumph and love will overcome evil, then the tragic is located and made less overwhelming.

It was Karl Marx who worried that a belief in life after death became a strategy used by the powerful to keep the powerless and marginalized under control. In Christian theology, the idea of life after death is the opposite. It is intended to force us to recognize a standard of how society should be ordered, which is a pressure on the present age. When we pray in the Lord's Prayer "your kingdom come," it is an invitation to recognize that the Christian hope of a life to come is a hope that we need to start to realize here and now.

Additional question: What do you imagine life after death looks like?

Do Episcopalians believe in hell?

When most people think about hell, they tend to think of a place of everlasting torment and punishment for those who are not Christians. This picture of hell probably owes more to Dante's *Divine Comedy* and Milton's *Paradise Lost*. Images of hell include literal flames, a frozen continent, and even poisonous snakes. The biblical basis for such a destination is grounded in the Hebrew concept of "Sheol" and the Greek concept of "Gehenna." Sheol in Hebrew thought tends to be a shadowy, half-existence for the departed, while Gehenna is closer to a place of punishment. Perhaps the Gospel that provides most of the material for the traditional picture of hell is the Gospel of Matthew (cf. Matthew 13:42; Matthew 25:30).

It is clear that the New Testament does teach that there is a sense in which each life will be held accountable for the use of our time on earth. However, there are many New Testament themes that challenge the traditional picture of hell. The God revealed in the life, death, and resurrection of Jesus is a God that loves us regardless of where we are; it is a God that will not let us escape God's loving embrace; it is a God that doesn't give up on any of us.

In addition, Christians believe that Christ died for the whole world. There are plenty of theologians in the tradition who suspected that in the end God's love gets through to everyone. God is ultimately irresistible.

You will find a spectrum of opinion among Episcopalians. Some on the more evangelical end of the spectrum will take the view that judgment is a significant biblical theme and therefore a reality for those who continue to resist the love of God, although even here there is a growing emphasis on the grace and mercy of God. Some on the more liberal end of the spectrum tend to the view that ultimately God's grace receives and welcomes us all.

In recent years, there has been a growth in popularity of the idea of a purgatory. In traditional Roman Catholic theology, it played a distinctive role of purgation for sin not yet absolved appropriately; in wider Protestant theology, it is the idea that for some lives we will need a little more time to discover the centrality of love before we can enjoy the intimacy of heaven. The best illustration of this was the Anglican C. S. Lewis, who in his book *The Great Divorce* described the possibility of transition from a state of complete self-preoccupation to love-centered reality. This transition, for Lewis, was the idea of purgatory.

Most Episcopalians tend to the view that God is much more surprising and generous than we expect. Therefore heaven will have plenty of occupants who will surprise us.

Additional question: Who do you expect to see in heaven?

What does it mean to say that humanity is made in the "image of God"?

In Genesis 1:26–27, we read:

> Then God said, "Let us make humankind in our image, according to our likeness; and let them have dominion over the fish of the sea, and over the birds of the air, and over the cattle, and over all the wild animals of the earth, and over every creeping thing that creeps upon the earth." So God created humankind in his image, in the image of God he created them; male and female he created them.

This text explains the distinctive status of every human being. We are made in the "image of God"—often referred to in the Latin as "*Imago Dei*." Every person is special. It means that we are all required to treat people with dignity. They are extraordinary creations of infinite worth.

But there is more to this doctrine. We are all made in such a way that we reflect the creator. Now this does not mean that God has a physical body, but that the capacity for relationship and rationality, coupled with the gift of moral discernment, are grounded in God and reflected in humanity. One of the reasons why we have a distinctive relationship with the environment is that we have these God-given capacities.

This means that we have a responsibility for the creation. It is precisely because we have the rational capacity to organize the world around us in certain ways that we must make sure that we exercise our power in ways that are respectful of the world in which we live.

Our purpose for being is to discover love. Discovering love means arriving at rightly ordered relationships with God (the source of everything that is on whom our existence depends), with nature (that which we must respect and seek to live in harmony with), and with each other. This purpose is made possible by the truth that humanity is created in the image of God.

Additional question: What does it mean to think that all people are special because they are made in the image of God?

What is sin? Do Episcopalians believe in original sin?

Part of the Christian understanding of humanity is the idea that human propensities for egoism, selfishness, and destructive relationships are found in every human being. Sin is the technical word used to describe these propensities. And the doctrine of original sin is an assertion of its universal nature. Although Episcopalians don't always use this language, it is widely agreed that the reality of sin and the fact that everyone is sinful is recognized as a truth about humans in society.

It is important to remember the divine project in creating this world was to create an environment where humans can discover the significance of love. Given this, we are all made with the capacity to either respond to love or resist love. Love cannot be compelled. It is perfectly possible to program a computer that tells you how much it loves you, but this is not love. True love cannot be programmed. The reason why the moment when a child expresses love toward a parent is so precious is precisely because the response is not programmed. The child is discovering what he or she means to give and receive love. This is only possible in a world where one can refuse to give and receive love.

The truth about love is that so many of us have deep ambivalence about making love central. We fear that we will be exploited; we are scared of being vulnerable; we don't want the inconvenience of being there for other people. So we start establishing patterns where self is central and others are there to be used.

Christian theology assumes that all humans, as we embark on the love project, will find it difficult. We will all struggle with our deep-seated tendencies to insist on self being the priority. This is the doctrine of original sin. For Christians, this is one of those empirical doctrines—there is lots of evidence in the world that this is true.

Unlike some other Christian traditions, the language of sin and original sin does not dominate our preaching. However, in our liturgy, we do make confession of sin central. In fact, in almost every service, there will be an opportunity to pause and reflect on our constant challenge to discover love and live love.

Additional question: In what ways do you find that you struggle to be loved centered rather than self centered?

What is the Episcopalian view of humanity? Are people basically good or bad?

For some Christian traditions, humans are depraved. There is nothing that we can do that is good. We are constantly prone to self-destructive patterns; even our efforts at being good are often driven by destructive self-interest. On this view, there is nothing good in us.

In reaction to this, there are other thinkers, such as Matthew Fox, who believe this picture of humanity is very destructive. It was the atheist thinker Feuerbach who suspected that we are inclined to project into the skies all the good virtues and leave all the bad vices with humanity. Matthew Fox has argued we need to recognize that we are fundamentally good.

Episcopalians tend to more sympathetic to the classical Roman Catholic line, which states that we are both created in the image of God (therefore fundamentally good and open to good impulses and virtuous behavior) and, at the same time, fallen (therefore flawed and constantly struggle with destructive patterns of behavior). It is because we are all made in the image of God that persons who know nothing about Christ and are outside the church are still able to be heroic, kind, and compassionate; it is because we are all sinful that everyone (both in the church and outside the church) can be irrationally destructive and cruel.

So we are basically good, yet flawed. We have both good inclination and bad inclination (to take a Jewish concept). And the invitation of the Gospel is to discover that God has provided the grace through Christ to live a life focused on love and to develop our better selves through the agency of the Holy Spirit.

Additional question: Why are some people worse than others? Do you think most people could do really wicked things?

Do Episcopalians believe in the atonement?

The word "atonement" literally means "at-one-ment." We are attempting to make sense of the significance of Jesus dying on the cross. The key idea which has inspired countless Christians is that in the end our relationship with the God of holiness and love is not dependent on our piety or ethical behavior, but upon what God has done for us in Christ. We are not required to meet unreachable standards, but simply accept the offer of "grace" (the undeserved merit and favor of God).

For many Christians the problem with the atonement is precisely how it works. Why should Jesus dying on the cross make any difference to my relationship with God? One thing is clear, this is not an uncomplicated biblical theme. In Romans 5, St. Paul explains, "But God proves his love for us in that while we still were sinners Christ died for us" (Romans 5:8).

Interestingly, the church never made the atonement a matter for the creeds. Instead, it allowed a proliferation of images, which are embedded in the New Testament, to develop in their distinctive ways. So the sacrifice texts of Scripture (e.g., Hebrews 10:11–13) were used by St. Augustine of Hippo (354–430) for the idea that the death of Jesus was a sacrifice to God offered by God to Godself (Godself is used when we are trying to avoid him or herself). Anselm (1033–1109) then took the ransom text from the Gospel of Mark (Mark 10:45) and suggested that Jesus is the one who pays the debt, by taking on himself the punishment that humanity is due. And it was Martin Luther (1483–1546) who built on the images of the death of Christ being a triumph over sin, death, hell, and Satan. Finally, Peter Abelard (1079–1142) took the language of Paul in Corthinians "Be imitators of me, as I am of Christ" (1 Corinthians 11:1) and suggested that primarily the death of Jesus on the cross is an efficacious example of God's love for humanity.

On the whole, Episcopalians are pleased that the Church didn't explicitly require Christians to believe a particular theory of the atonement. Many are very aware of the problems with the idea: Why can't God just forgive humanity their sins? How come Satan has "rights" over the sinner? However, for many Episcopalians, the idea that our inadequate attempts to realize a loving way of being are not the condition of salvation is important; and the idea that God transforms our sinful predicament through grace is indeed the message of salvation.

More recently, certain Anglican theologians, for example, Vernon White, have suggested that a good way to look at the atonement is to see the cross as giving God the authority to forgive. When Nelson Mandela came out of prison in South Africa, he called on the black victims of white oppression to be generous and forgiving to their oppressors. Mandela had the authority to do this because he was a victim of white oppression. By analogy, the God Man dying on the cross enables God to forgive the unspeakable crimes that humans inflict on each other because God has been a victim of those crimes.

For most Episcopalians, we want to find a way to embrace the idea without committing ourselves to a particular theory of how God is able to save.

Additional question: In what sense does Jesus save for you?

What do Episcopalians believe about the end of the world?

We live in a time where there is considerable interest and speculation in the end of the world. It is also a significant biblical theme. Eschatology is the technical term for the study of the "end times." The expectation that Jesus will return is embedded in our creeds. So the question: How should we understand this idea?

Episcopalians are interested in learning about the truth from wherever that truth can be found. We are open to a range of conversation partners. So let us start thinking about this question by looking at what the scientists say.

From a scientific perspective, the end of the universe is not imminent. Any scenario about the entire universe is tens of billions of years in the future. From a cosmological perspective, the more immediate problem is our sun. In about four billion years, the hydrogen from the core of our star will get depleted and our star will slowly die. Given it is difficult to get off this planet, it looks likely that humanity is doomed to extinction.

Now this picture of the universe contrasts very markedly with the picture painted by the authors of the famous Left Behind series. This was a series of novels that sketched out the rapture (when the truly born again disappear to be removed from the coming tribulations), then the emergence of the Antichrist and the gradual battle culminating in Armageddon. For Tim LaHaye and Jerry B. Jenkins (the authors of the Left Behind series), all the signs of the end are around us. The rapture will, in their view, happen any day now.

Most Anglican theologians want to distance themselves from both the immanence of the Left Behind narrative and the pessimism of the scientific narrative. The problem with the Left Behind narrative is that it imposes a system called dispensationalism on Scripture, which is not really found in Scripture. Dispensationalism is the division of human history into seven ages, which includes dividing the Second Coming of Jesus into two stages. It was invented in the nineteenth century by John Nelson Darby; and the whole schema is not really found in Scripture. The problem with the pessimism of the scientific narrative is that it ignores the Christian conviction that God is active in creation. In the same way that God used a Big Bang to enable life to emerge, so God will work with the forces of nature at the end of the age to ensure the triumph of love and complete arrival of God's kingdom.

As we saw with evolution, we have modified our understanding about the origins of the world. Episcopalians do not think that the world started in 4004 BCE, but agree with the scientific consensus that the world started 13.7 billion years ago. So we need to make a similar shift in time scale with the end of the age. Instead of speculating endlessly on the whether the world will end tomorrow or next year or the year after next, we should adjust our heads, in the light of the science, to recognize that the chances are the world will continue for some time to come.

For Episcopalians, we worry much more about what we should be doing to bring us closer to the reign of God that Scripture promises at the end of the age, than in trying to predict a date and time when the end of the age is going to occur.

Additional question: Why do you think people enjoy speculating about the end of the age so much?

Ethics

How do Episcopalians decide what is right and wrong in ethics?

In the first section, we looked at the same question in respect to theology. How do Episcopalians decide what is right and wrong in theology? In many ways, this question provokes a similar answer. We are committed to the conviction that in Jesus Christ we see God. If you want to know what God is like, then you need to look at the "words and actions" of Jesus of Nazareth. The Anglican biblical scholar Richard Burridge explains that the very purpose of each Gospel is to invite us to imitate the "words and deeds" of Jesus.[1] As we live lives modeled on the life of Jesus, so we become agents of love in the world.

Jesus is the touchstone on our ethics. This means that Episcopalians consider any ethical system grounded on hate (for example, white supremacy or anti-Semitism) clearly incompatible with what we learn about God in Jesus. However, there are issues that are much harder to determine. Does the Jesus touchstone mean that all war is wrong? Does the Jesus touchstone forbid divorce and remarriage? Does the Jesus touchstone mean that infertility treatments are inappropriate? To Episcopalians, it looks like God wanted to set us in a direction, but also wanted us to work in community to discern the truth about some of these harder topics.

The work of discernment is similar to the process in theology. We study Scripture very carefully; we listen to the voices that make up our tradition; we seek to discern what we can learn from science; we listen with care to the experiences of those who are so easily marginalized and

---

1. Richard Burridge, *Imitating Jesus*, (Grand Rapids: Eerdmans, 1997).

excluded; and we offer our understanding with some humility, ready and willing to revise our understanding as new information comes to light.

This means that the Episcopal Church is willing to live with a range of positions on certain questions. We value the range of perspectives. The act of ensuring that there are a range of perspectives ensures that we are always sensitive to questions and objections in our positions. We live with mystery; we are not always seeking to "solve" all the questions.

Although we recognize that the task of discerning the truth means that sometimes our understanding of the truth is approximate, we still insist that there is a truth to discover. Moral theologians in the Episcopal Church are in agreement: ethics is a matter of discovery, not invention. We are seeking to discover what God really wants. We are not inventing what we would like. In the same way that some issues in science are clear (e.g., the law of gravity) and other issues are less clear (e.g., the nature of black holes), so Episcopalians see that some issues are clear (e.g., the obscenity of racism) and other issues are less clear (e.g., the legitimacy of a just war). With the issues that are less clear, we are required to be in community, struggling and grappling with these issues.

Additional question: Which ethical issues do you think are clear and which ones less so?

Do Episcopalians allow birth control?

The Episcopal Church does allow married couples to use contraception. The Episcopal Church has mirrored the gradual shift that has happened across the entire Anglican Communion. It was the Lambeth Conference of 1930 (the meeting of all the Anglican Bishops in the Communion) which conceded that there might be certain circumstances where contraception might be appropriate. However, by the Lambeth Conference of 1958, there was a recognition that the purposes of sexual intimacy are not confined to procreation. In the Garden of Eden, God says, "It is not good that the man should be alone" (Genesis 2:18). This text means that an important aspect to sexual intimacy is the privilege of being close to someone. The Episcopal Church in 1994 directed dioceses and agencies to "provide information to all men and women on the full range of affordable, acceptable, safe, and non coercive contraceptive and reproductive health care services."[2]

---

2. General Convention Resolution 1994-A054 *http://www.episcopalarchives.org/cgi-bin/ acts/acts_resolution.pl?resolution=1994-A054* (accessed November 12, 2013).

The responsible use of birth control, within a loving and committed marriage, is both approved and endorsed by the Episcopal Church.

Additional question: Do you think that some methods of birth control are more appropriate than others?

Why is marriage important in the Episcopal Church?

Christians are in agreement about the importance and centrality of marriage as the basis of the family. For centuries, Christians have recognized that a child needs to be born within a context of two loving parents who are going to stick together and be there for this child who, in the normal course of events, will outlive the parents. We share with Roman Catholics the view that it is a sacramental rite. Sacraments are vehicles of grace, which are given by Christ. To describe marriage as a sacramental rite is to recognize that when a couple enters into a lifelong union and make their vows in front of God and the congregation, they receive blessing and grace from God. We believe it mirrors the love that Christ has for her church.

The Episcopal Church recognizes that some people are called to live as a single person—sometimes out of choice, sometimes forced on them by the inability to find a life partner. We celebrate the delightful contribution that a single person can make in the life of the Church. A friend who is single is often a great godparent to a child. Congregations in the Episcopal Church love having men and women who are able to give generously of their time to support program and activities.

Marriage is a serious undertaking. It is normal for a couple who are getting married in the Episcopal Church to undergo a course for marriage preparation. We believe a couple should talk through the sensitive and complex issues surrounding sex and money. It is also important to discuss such questions as: How are we going to divide time between the two families during the holidays? It is also important to have the same basic outlook to raising a child.

Marriage can be so life enhancing. For Episcopalians, it is an extraordinary gift from God.

Additional question: Some people are choosing not to get married but just "live together" instead. What do you think are the advantages of marriage over living together?

What does the Episcopal Church think about divorce and remarriage?

For some people, marriage does not work out. Their intentions were good, but due to complex factors, the marriage dies. Now the Episcopal Church does not use the language of annulment (i.e., the view that there was never an authentic marriage there in the first place). Instead, the Episcopal Church takes the view that people can make every effort, but find in the complexity of living the marriage becoming increasingly destructive on all the parties involved.

At this point, the Episcopal Church recognizes that God can take tragic and hard situations and transform them into situations of grace and hope. God can forgive our failings and create new options for the future. Therefore grounded in our confidence about the agency of God to create a new chance for a monogamous and committed relationship to be granted to the divorced person, the Episcopal Church allows persons who are divorced to remarry and live a full life within the Church.

There is a process within the Episcopal Church for a person who is divorced to get remarried. Normally, the priest is required to petition the bishop. Sometimes, if there have been several divorces, the bishop may require the couple to involve a counselor. The goal is simple: we are committed to the ideal that marriage is lifelong; and we want to make sure that this new marriage succeeds.

Additional question: How do you think the Episcopal Church can support a person who is divorced to succeed in their subsequent marriage?

Where does the Episcopal Church stand on homosexuality?

Where contraception was the challenge facing the church during the early to the middle of the twentieth century, the status of two people of the same gender who are attracted to each other is the issue of our day. As the church of the twentieth century had to discern what is right about contraception, we are being called to discern what "holy living" looks like for all Christians, including our gay and lesbian brothers and sisters.

Almost everyone recognizes that same sex attraction is not a matter of choice. Although we are not sure about the precise science behind sexual attraction in general, we do know that some people have deep and sustained attractions to a person of the same gender that is part of their identity. We now recognize that there are sexual orientations.

Armed with this information about our gay and lesbian brothers and sisters, the church then needs to reflect on how to put this information into conversation with Scripture and the Christian tradition. We learn from Scripture that human sexuality is part of the creation, which God declared was good. We learn that Jesus wants men and women to be in committed, lifelong, monogamous relationships. So perhaps the church needs to welcome our gay and lesbian brothers and sisters into the same type of relationships.

There are a small number of texts in the Bible that imply that homosexuality is inappropriate and wrong. Naturally, none of these texts were aware of what we now know about sexual orientations. St. Paul in Romans 1 seems to describing persons who are heterosexual in orientation deciding to indulge in homosexual acts (Romans 1:27) and the extraordinary episode of homosexual rape in Sodom (Genesis 19) are not the same as two men or two women who are committed to each other and want to express their love for each other physically.

As a result of this process of discernment, the Episcopal Church does allow gay and lesbian persons to be priests and bishops. And some dioceses in the Episcopal Church permit gay and lesbian couples to use the new same-sex blessing rite and have their relationship celebrated and affirmed. Naturally, there are those who feel that sexual intimacy should be confined to a traditional marriage between one man and one woman. Their voice in the church is welcomed. We need the perspectives of both liberals and conservatives.

Additional question: What factors do you think need to be taken into account as the Church discerns the appropriate ethic for human sexuality?

Why does social justice matter so much to the Episcopal Church?

If you had to identity the single most important biblical theme, then I think any fair observer would say "social justice." It is the primary theme of the Gospel (Jesus never mentions homosexuality, but talks repeatedly about the dangers of riches and the importance of the poor); it is the major theme of the prophets in the Old Testament (just look at Isaiah, Amos, and Micah); and it is a central characteristic of the early church (see Acts 4:33–35). The Episcopal Church is a biblical church; and this commitment is firmly embedded in Scripture.

The Church is called to be an agent of change in society. So you will find almost all Episcopal churches have significant outreach programs. Feeding the homeless, opening the building for the Alcoholics Anonymous group, organizing a mission trip, supporting Habitat for Humanity—all these programs and more can be found in your typical Episcopal church.

Some feel that such a commitment is "political." It is not intended to be party political. Specialists in Christian Ethics in the Episcopal Church are well aware that strategies for overcoming poverty are a matter of legitimate political debate: the right will argue that a strong, robust market economy generates wealth for everyone and this will do the most to overcome poverty; and the left tends to argue that government programs are essential to overcome poverty. The witness of the Church is that a priority must always be those who are excluded. The best way of serving social justice is a matter of legitimate debate.

Additional question: In what ways does your church witness to the importance of social justice?

Where does the Episcopal Church stand on issues like abortion and euthanasia?

These are highly sensitive questions. Both of these issues relate to an important commitment that all Christians share, namely the sanctity of life. Abortion is seen as the taking of a developing human life in the womb; euthanasia is seen as the termination of a human life for the elderly or terminally ill.

On abortion, at the General Convention of 1994, the Episcopal Church stated: "While we acknowledge that in this country it is the legal right of every woman to have a medically safe abortion, as Christians we believe strongly that if this right is exercised, it should be used only in extreme situations. We emphatically oppose abortion as a means of birth control, family planning, sex selection, or any reason of mere convenience."[3] This carefully worded statement recognizes

---

3. General Convention 1994 A054 *http://www.episcopalarchives.org/cgi-bin/acts/acts_ resolution.pl?resolution=1994-A054* (accessed November 12, 2013).

the decision of the Supreme Court that a woman should be able to make medical decisions for her body in consultation with the doctrine (Roe v. Wade 1973), but invites the woman to only make this decision in "extreme situations."

It was at the same General Convention the Episcopal Church clarified its position on euthanasia. Here the resolution declared: "It is morally wrong and unacceptable to intentionally take a human life in order to relieve the suffering caused by incurable illness. This would include the intentional shortening of another person's life by the use of a lethal dose of medication or poison, the use of lethal weapons, homicidal acts, and other forms of active euthanasia. Palliative treatment to relieve the pain of persons with progressive incurable illnesses, even if done with the knowledge that a hastened death may result, is consistent with theological tenets regarding the sanctity of life."[4] The line being taken here is that to take deliberately a person's life is wrong. However, sometimes a doctor, when managing a person's pain, does increase the medication that may hasten death and this is morally acceptable. In a situation of pain management, a palliative care specialist does point out that this pain management might increase the length of life, even if death is inevitable due to the dose, because pain can also hasten death. Provided the intent is to manage pain, the Episcopal Church does consider such action as morally acceptable.

These resolutions do illustrate how the Episcopal Church has attempted to respect the commitment the Church has to safeguard the sanctity of human life, yet recognize that both at the beginning and end of lives there are complexities that need appropriate medical action.

Naturally, there are Episcopalians who would like to see the Church take a different position—either more restricted or more progressive. As on many issues, we continue to be in moral discernment.

Additional question: Do you think the Episcopal Church is taking a liberal or conservative position on these questions?

---

4. General Convention 1994-A056 *http://www.episcopalarchives.org/cgi-bin/acts/acts_resolution.pl?resolution=1994-A056* (accessed November 12, 2013).

Can a Christian fight in a war?

Christians are called to be peacemakers. We are called to witness to love and to invite everyone to find ways of living together. This is our primary gospel obligation. However, from time to time, we find ourselves in situations where it seems that the creation of a just peace needs to involve the exercise of force. During the Second World War, Adolf Hitler did not appear to be interested in a just peace—he just wanted surrender. The result was a brutal war, where many lives were lost.

This is another area of difficult discernment. In the Old Testament, there are plenty of wars that God appears to sanction. In the New Testament, we have the robust witness of Jesus that seems to call us to be willing to absorb the violence that others want to inflict. In the Sermon on the Mount (Matthew 5–7), Jesus instructs his disciples to take not what we are entitled to (one eye for one eye), but to break the cycle of violence. We see around the world too many communities that descend into revenge killing—one wrong leads to a revenge killing, which leads to another revenge killing and so it continues. Jesus wants love to triumph over revenge; he did not simply advocate this pacifist ethic, but lived it. He was in a political setting in a country under occupation. In this setting, he was willing to die at the hands of the occupying power, rather than participate in a violent struggle.

This is another area of legitimate disagreement. We have the entire spectrum of opinion in the Church. At one of the end of the spectrum are those who are pacifists. They would argue that the distinctive Christian witness is that violence as a means of resolving conflicts is always wrong. At the other end of the spectrum are those who think that occasionally, as a last resort, the only way to bring about a just peace is the legitimate exercise of force.

Additional question: Do you think, as a Christian, that sometimes the government should be allowed to go to war?

Where do Episcopalians stand on the environment?

Generalizations about Episcopalians are tricky. On almost all questions, there is a range of answers. The General Convention of the Episcopal Church has expressed a deep concern for the environment. Given it is a tradition that takes the witness of science very seriously, it is not surprising that climate change, in particular, has figured prominently.

The reason why these positions have arisen is simple. There is a clear biblical obligation to care for the environment. The dramatic drama in the early chapters of Genesis set forth the parameters. Into an environment which God, at the end of Genesis 1 declares is "good," humanity is placed. Humans are given "stewardship," which means we are called to take care of the world around us. This world that God has declared is good must be appropriately maintained so it is good for the future generations.

An environmental ethic is one that recognizes that we owe certain obligations to the future. We must ensure that future generations are still able to obtain fresh water, enjoy beautiful scenery, use certain energy resources, and appreciate the rich and diverse nature of the animal and plant realms.

Some in the green movement think that too often Christians only see the environment in terms of "humans." Some have called this a "shallow ecology." Instead of a "shallow ecology," they want a "deep ecology," which recognizes the intrinsic rights of all living organisms to exist. So animals, fish, plants, and trees do not simply exist for humanity's benefit, but in their own right.

Some Episcopalians are sympathetic to this critique. They do want to talk about "animal rights" or even the "rights of a tree or waterfall." However, most Episcopalians feel that it is important to recognize that some living entities have greater rights than other entities. So a human is more important than a dog; and a dog is more important than a carrot; and the AIDS virus has absolutely no rights at all.

Finally, most congregations are involved in recycling and reusing. In many ways, this is simply a recovery of a post–World War II ethic of "avoid waste." Waste is so tragic: it is expensive and hard work to eliminate. Taking a moment to enable the newspaper to be recycled or the plastic shopping bag to be reused is just an act of a responsible citizen.

Additional question: Do you see caring for the environment as a faith issue?

Why am I obligated to get involved in civic society?

The Anglican tradition has a positive view of the state. Some Christian groups are much more skeptical, but Anglicans believe that it is good if society is shaped by faith values. We think it is important to keep a deep connection between the state and the church. This was one of the reasons why in 1893 an Act of Congress approved the decision of the Episcopal Church to build the Washington National Cathedral.

The Episcopal Church places a high value on community. We believe that humans are intended to be social. When we talk about the body of Christ, we are talking about a community that is intrinsically connected—every part of the body is essential from the smallest figure to the largest organ. And one role of the body of Christ is to be the presence of Christ in the world.

Part of being the presence of Christ is involvement in civic society. We are obliged to vote and participate in the political structures of society. We should join and get involved in neighborhood associations. Trade unions and volunteer associations are important. We do all this because society needs the faith perspective. We need to get involved in political and civic organizations. We need to support such organizations by volunteering and helping them obtain resources.

People of faith are at the heart of many volunteer organizations. And faith is often the motivation. Inspired by our Lord's words in Matthew 25, we want to be there to make a difference: we want to see the hungry fed, the homeless housed, and the prisoner visited. We are called to see Christ in others through this outreach ministry. For Anglicans, this is the work of mission.

Katharine Jefferts Schori (who became the presiding bishop in 2006) made the Anglican "five marks of mission" central to her understanding of mission. These marks are:

- To proclaim the Good News of the kingdom
- To teach, baptize, and nurture new believers
- To respond to human need with loving service
- To seek to transform unjust structures of society
- To strive to safeguard the integrity of creation, and sustain and renew the life of the earth.

Episcopalians are an involved crowd. You will find many civic organizations have Episcopalians in leadership roles. It is because there is an intrinsic Anglican obligation to be involved.

Additional question: In what ways are you involved in society?

What should be my attitude toward money and wealth?

Just a cursory glance at the Gospels makes one realize that Jesus had lots to say about the relationship of discipleship to wealth. Repeatedly those who wish to follow Jesus are instructed to "go and sell everything they have and give to the poor." The vision Jesus has for his disciples is that they "trust" in God to provide and serve those who are in need around them. Like all Christians, the Episcopal Church struggles with these texts. We are forced to recognize that a deep attachment to money and wealth is sinful. It is so easy to embark on the project of creating a financial safety net that covers every conceivable eventuality; it is also so misguided. Life is fragile. Stock markets can crash; housing values can evaporate; banks can go bankrupt; businesses can fail. Instead of living with this perpetual anxiety, Jesus invites us to live in a community of mutual support. Give to others and, when things are hard for you, others will give to you. Instead of opting for self-support, Jesus invites us into the church, where we should find a network for mutual support.

This means that Episcopalians are called to be generous. We are invited to really trust God; we are invited to really trust that others will be there when the inconceivable and horrendous happens. Generosity is an important part of our discipleship.

Naturally supporting our local church is important; however, our generosity should extend far beyond the local congregation. We need to support the arts, education, and outreach programs. And we need to remember that we are part of a global Anglican family. Our brothers and sisters elsewhere on the globe also need our support. Getting use to writing out checks is an important part of being a member of the Episcopal Church.

Additional question: How seriously do you take the invitation of Jesus to be trust God and be generous with the resources that God has given you?

Church Architecture and Vestments

Why can't you just worship God in a big warehouse?

You can worship God anywhere. And you can find Episcopal congregations in all sorts of different types of buildings. However, it is true that the overwhelming majority of Episcopal congregations worship in a church building which has been dedicated to the worship of God. And you will find that when you worship in a dedicated building for worship, you can, if you sit still just for a moment, feel the prayer-drenched walls that surround you.

In addition, when a building has been consecrated for the worship of God, you will find that there are plenty of mechanisms built in to help us focus on God. It is very easy to let our minds wander; in an Episcopal Church, it is harder. Often there is stained glass, which tells the story of the life of faith. (This was the reason why stained glass emerged in church buildings—it was an educational device for people who could not read and write.) There will most often be a large cross, which is a reminder of the key theme of our faith, namely, God suffered and died on a cross. There is almost always an altar (typically called the Communion Table), which points to the central significance of the Eucharist (the shared supper of bread and wine) in our tradition. At least one place (sometimes two) for the preaching and proclamation of the Word (i.e., the Bible) will be equally prominent. And often as you walk into the space, you will pass the font. This is the place of baptism, where we are reminded anew of our promises to live as faithful disciples of Christ.

The idea is that the architecture is part of the message. Through the design and shape of the building, we learn about our faith. The architecture is intended to help us focus on what matters—the worship of God.

Additional question: Next time you are in an Episcopal Church, take a moment to notice where things are. Why do you think this particular church has organized the space in this particular way?

What are the various parts of an Episcopal Church called?

Although there are a whole variety of different Episcopal church buildings, it is striking how similar so many of these buildings are. In the majority of church buildings, you will arrive at the narthex (this is the space at the entrance to the church where the procession can form and visitors are welcomed). As you look into the church, the inside is often cruciform in shape (i.e., it is shaped like a cross). The heart of the church is the nave—this is where the people sit facing the altar. At the sides (making up the arms of the cross shape) are the transepts (often, incidentally, a good place to sit—you are nearer the action). Toward the front of the church is the sanctuary (this is the home of the altar). Near the sanctuary, there is sometimes a chancel. This is often where the altar party sits (the group of acolytes—those who help with the liturgy, especially assisting the deacon, if there is one, to set the table; the crucifer—the person who carries the cross; and the presider—the celebrant who celebrates or presides at the table). It is called a sanctuary because it is a place of holy action, where in the miracle of the Eucharist the grace of God comes afresh to the people of God.

Additional question: Do you think guests are aware of the organization of the church building? How could we explain it more clearly?

Why do all the participants in the service vest?

The work of worship is holy work. And those who are participating in leading the worship are often expected to wear distinctive attire. The primary color is white—a color symbolic of purity. Probably the basic attire for Holy Eucharist is the alb, which originally was simply a tunic worn by the citizens of ancient Rome. Sometimes this is tied around the waist with a cincture. Then for the priest, there is a stole, which is a strip of cloth (often in the color of the church season) that is hung around the neck. The deacon wears the stole diagonally across the body. Often the priest who is celebrating the Eucharist will wear a chasuble (an outer vestment that is normally in the color that represents the season of the church year) on top of the alb.

At a service of Morning or Evening Prayer, you will often find the participants wearing a cassock with surplice. For some, the simplicity of the attire is more appropriate for worship. The cassock is often black and double breasted.

Often in an Episcopal church, you will find choir members and acolytes also wear a surplice (which is a white tunic) worn over a cassock. The total effect of all this distinctive attire is to invite us to appreciate the significance and privilege of worship. Most events and activities require distinctive attire—you wear soccer gear to play soccer and black tie when at an important reception or dinner. So at church, those who are playing an important role in the leading of worship dress appropriately.

Additional question: What impact does it have on you as you watch the procession of all these people in different attire?

Scripture

How important is the Bible to Episcopalians?

Episcopalians have at times been called a "people of the book," but the book in question is usually not the Bible, but the Book of Common Prayer. While other Christian churches have Bibles in the pews, the pews in Episcopal churches generally contain Prayer Books and hymnals instead. And it is a rare instance when you see individual Episcopalians bringing their own Bible to Sunday worship, much less have it contain notes and markings from ongoing personal and group study, though this is a common occurrence in some other Christian traditions. An outsider might well surmise from observing these things that the Bible is not really that important to most Episcopalians. In fact, many Episcopalians might agree.

But such a conclusion would be incorrect. From the beginnings of our Anglican heritage, Thomas Cranmer infused the Prayer Book with Scripture. All of our "common prayer," he argued, must be grounded in the Bible, which "containeth all things necessary to salvation."[1] This affirmation would be forever enshrined in the ordination services, as every bishop, priest, and deacon solemnly declares: "I do believe the Holy Scriptures of the Old and New Testaments to be the Word of God, and to contain all things necessary to salvation."[2] There is much that we will never know or understand in this earthly life, but that which we do need both for our own spiritual well-being and for the redemption of the world is found within those precious pages. As Hymn 631 proclaims, "Book of books, our people's strength;

---

1. Book of Common Prayer, 868.
2. Book of Common Prayer, 513.

statesman's, teacher's, hero's treasure; bringing freedom, spreading truth, shedding light that none can measure."[3]

This is why our worship services are full of Scripture. The entire first half of the Eucharistic service, the "Liturgy of the Word," contains readings from the Old Testament, the Psalms, the Epistles, and the Gospels, along with a sermon based on all or some of the passages read. And beyond this, it is quickly obvious that biblical language is interwoven throughout the rest of the liturgy. From the opening acclamation to the final dismissal, Scripture is an important—no, essential—part of our worship, our "common prayer."

Additional question: How important is Holy Scripture to you?

What does it mean to say that the Bible is the Word of God?

The catechism at the back of the Prayer Book states, "We call the Holy Scriptures the Word of God because God inspired their human authors and because God still speaks to us through the Bible."[4] To say that God "inspired" the original authors does not imply that these individuals were somehow robots with buttons to push or puppets with strings to pull. There were dozens of contributors over literally a thousand years who wrote in vastly different styles. The common denominator is that they were, as 2 Timothy 3:16 says, "God-breathed." God's breath flows through those writings; God's Word is discovered within those human words.

This Bible, therefore, is no mere blueprint or owner's manual, much less just another old book—it is something far greater. The Bible is, as Frank Wade says in his book *Transforming Scripture*, our "meeting ground," where we can encounter God anew.[5] Through the same Spirit who inspired the original authors, the words on those pages we hold (or, in today's world, the words on our electronic reader!) communicate to us once more the living Word of God who, as John's Gospel states, "became flesh and lived among us" (1:14).

It can be helpful, therefore, to open each time of personal Bible reading or group study with a prayer. One helpful prayer is Collect 28

---

3. Hymnal 1982, 631

4. Book of Common Prayer, 853.

5. Frank Wade, *Transforming Scripture* (New York: Church Publishing 2008), 1.

in the Prayer Book (p. 236), which says, "Blessed Lord, who caused all holy Scriptures to be written for our learning: Grant us to so hear them, read, mark, learn, and inwardly digest them, that we may embrace and ever hold fast the blessed hope of everlasting life, which you have given us in our Savior Jesus Christ; who lives and reigns with you and the Holy Spirit, one God, for ever and ever. Amen."

This prayer reminds us that Scripture is not cotton candy to be swallowed easily, but something to be chewed on, wrestled with. From "In the beginning" in Genesis 1 to "Amen, come, Lord Jesus" in Revelation 22, the pages of our Bible form a continuous, but not always clear narrative. Discovering and understanding the inspired Word of God is not necessarily easy, and admittedly we Episcopalians often do not take the time to do the study that is needed. But it is always worth whatever efforts we put into the process.

Additional question: How have you encountered God when reading the Bible?

How many books are in an Episcopalian's Bible?

Although it is hard to imagine now, for the first few centuries after the time of Jesus—not years, centuries—there was no Christian Bible, no definitive set of canonical or authoritative texts. Indeed, there were actually many so-called gospels and epistles and other writings floating around, all claiming to speak with authority about God and Jesus. Some were more obviously uninspired than others, and were put aside quite easily! Some, like the Letter of Jude and the Revelation to John, had a tough time being accepted at first, but they eventually were accepted. Still others, like the Letter of Clement and the Teachings of the Twelve Apostles, came close but did not make it in, but have since been honored as part of a collection known as the "Apostolic Fathers." By the time a fourth-century bishop named Athanasius included in a letter a full list of twenty-seven "canonical"—or authoritative writings—the New Testament was complete. It is important to note that it was not because of his letter that these writings were accepted, but rather he was able to list them because the church's people had over time consistently heard God's Word through them.

Then there were the Hebrew Scriptures, the "bible" that Jesus himself knew and from which he quoted. Even here, however, there was some dispute about how many books comprised what Christians would come to call the "Old Testament." The thirty-nine books that are found in most Protestant Bibles today are the books that were originally written in Hebrew, including the Torah or Law (the first five books), the Prophets (like Isaiah and Jeremiah), and the Writings (like the Psalms or Proverbs). There were, however, other books written at a later time and in Greek, not Hebrew. These books (including 1 and 2 Maccabees, Judith, and Tobit) were accepted in some collections but not others. Because Jerome included them when he translated the Scriptures into Latin, Roman Catholic Bibles to this day contain these additional books in their Old Testament. In some modern Bibles, including those used by Episcopalians, these are distinguished from the thirty-nine undisputed books by calling them "Deutero-Canonical" or more commonly "the Apocrypha," and when read during worship services, they are not referred to as "The Word of the Lord" but simply as a "reading" or "lesson."

Additional question: Reflect on which books of the Bible are most important to you and why.

Do we take the Bible literally?

The short answer is that we as Episcopal Christians take the Bible very seriously—which is not the same thing as taking it literally.

More to the point, this means that we take seriously both the text of what we read and the context in which those words were written and subsequently received. It is not enough to read a verse of Scripture on its own, divorced from its setting in the larger passage. Sadly, there have been many times in the history of Christianity when people have wrenched a verse from its context and used it to justify otherwise deplorable acts such as slavery, racism, even crusades and inquisitions. Even in less extreme situations, it is far too easy either to take a verse that supports our own biases or to react against a too-easy fundamentalist approach by dismissing all of Scripture as irrelevant.

No, we choose to do the harder work. This means considering the passage surrounding a particular verse. What is the point of the larger piece, and how does that verse fit in it? What might the biblical author have been saying to the readers then, and why? This is where Bible studies, commentaries, and scholarly aids can prove very helpful. An important part of our Anglican heritage is the role that reason, not just tradition, has played in understanding Scripture and addressing changing situations. While affirming the way that Christians before us have comprehended the Word of God in relation to their time and place, we must also ask what God might be saying to us now in our own context.

This does not mean that anything goes—far from it. It does mean, as the prophets often reminded the people of Israel, that God can do a new thing if we are willing to let go of our own presuppositions and dare to approach both Scripture and our own situation with fresh eyes. As the apostle Paul said, we must wean ourselves off of spiritual milk, acknowledging that the goal is not easy answers, but a deeper appreciation of the presence and power of God in our midst, no matter what the circumstance.

Additional question: Which of my presuppositions may need to be challenged?

What about the difficult parts of the Bible?

Let's face it. If someone wanted to write a feel-good, easily understood, totally inspirational—not to mention G-rated—spiritual book, the Bible would probably not be it. After all, one does not have to tread far into the very first book, Genesis, before finding sex and violence and despicable acts. It is little surprise that some readers have found it all too easy to dismiss the Bible altogether based on troublesome passages that they come across. It is much like those who refuse to go to church because they say it is filled with so many hypocrites. The obvious response to this is: "Yes, but the good news is that there is always room for one more!" Likewise, we encourage people to read the Bible precisely because it is neither prefabricated nor simplistic, but instead reflects all of life in its pages—the good, the bad, and the ugly.

So how do we deal with these difficult passages when we encounter them? Everyone looks at the Scriptures through a lens of some kind. Our "lens" will subsequently help shape the way that we approach a given passage and ultimately interpret it. For example, considering those parts of Joshua or Judges that describe the wholesale slaughter of enemy populations, civilians and combatants alike, we can note that some Christians, including many during the Crusades, read such passages through the "lens" of a God of wrath, and thereby use the passages to justify their own violence against those they considered to be "infidels." For others, the "lens" of a God of unconditional love leads them to view those same passages of slaughter as examples of human-kind's fallen state and need for redemption.

Many Episcopalians have a "lens" that we call the Baptismal Covenant (see the Prayer Book, 304) by which we understand our actions as followers of Christ and approach the difficult biblical passages with this in mind. For others the "lens" might be the Anglican Five Marks of Mission (see the website of the Episcopal Church or the Anglican Communion), or the Nicene Creed (Prayer Book, 358), or simply John 3:16, "For God so loved the world . . ." All of these will shape how we read and comprehend the Scriptures.

Additional question: What is my "lens" through which I approach the Bible?

Do Episcopalians study the Bible?

Every ten years, bishops from throughout the worldwide Anglican Communion (including those from the Episcopal Church) gather together for prayer, fellowship, and deliberation on all manner of issues in what is known as the Lambeth Conference. At their meeting in 1998, they passed a resolution inviting member churches "to promote at every level biblical study programs which can inform and nourish the life of dioceses, congregations, seminaries, communities, and members of all ages" (Resolution III.1.c—go to *www.lambeth conference.org*).

Many Episcopalians have indeed sought out such study opportunities. Seasonal small group studies, such as in Lent, continue to thrive in many congregations, while more ambitious programs such as the four-year certificate program called Education for Ministry, or EFM, attract lay people who want to go deeper. In recent years, the Center for Biblical Studies has introduced "the Bible Challenge," providing a method by which individuals, congregations, and dioceses can read through the entire Bible. A link to this program is found on the Episcopal Church's website.

Then there are printed and online aids for study, most notably Forward Movement's Forward Day by Day booklets, as well as various publications through The Episcopal Network for Stewardship (TENS). Other programs and methods, including Disciples of Christ in Community (DOCC), Lectio Divina, the Alpha Course, and African Bible Study, are surveyed in Frank Wade's *Transforming Scripture*.

There is also the lectionary curriculum *Living the Good News*, which has been popular and well used for over thirty years. And for worshipping communities in need of Bibles due to financial difficulties, the Bible and Common Prayer Book Society has long been a faithful supplier at no charge. A project commissioned by the Anglican Consultative Council in 2009, entitled "The Bible in the Life of the Church," explores how we as Anglicans actually use the Bible in different parts of the Communion and also provides actual resource materials on a Communion-wide level.

Episcopalians may not always make use of these resources, but for those who wish, the opportunities abound for the people in the pews, and for the leadership of the Church and the global Communion. It is heartening to note that at the 2008 Lambeth Conference the bishops themselves modeled what they had encouraged a decade earlier, as they eschewed legislative sessions and resolutions and instead met in small groups for prayer, conversation, and, yes, Bible study.

Additional question: How could you incorporate intentional Bible study into your life?

What versions of the Bible do Episcopalians accept and use?

In 1538, Sir Thomas Cromwell, secretary to King Henry VIII and vicar general, directed the clergy of the Church of England, now fully independent from the Church of Rome, to provide in their churches "one book of the Bible of the largest volume in English," and to make sure it would be set up in a convenient place so that parishioners could "most commodiously resort to the same and read it."[6] That book was the Great Bible, so named because of its large size, and contained in its second edition a preface written by Henry's archbishop of Canterbury and author of the Book of Common Prayer, Thomas Cranmer. In that preface, Cranmer spoke of the importance of having the Bible available "in the vulgar tongue," namely, in English and not Latin, so that individual members of the Church "would not lack the fruit of reading."[7] That book became the first of many English translations through the centuries.

---

6. Thomas Cromwell, "Injunction of 1538," as found at *http://www.bl.uk/onlinegallery/onlineex/henryviii/musspowor/greatbible/index.html* (accessed November 1, 2013).

7. Thomas Cranmer, "Preface to the Great Bible," 1539.

Today, there are many English-language translations of the Scriptures. Perhaps the best known of these is the Authorized Version of the Bible, more commonly called the King James Bible. It is this version that historically was used by Episcopalians and other Christians, and it is still the version found in hotel rooms, thanks to the Gideon organization. Several other, often more readable, versions have been authorized through the years by the General Convention for use within the Episcopal Church. These include:

English Revision (1881)
American Revision (1901)
Revised Standard Version (1952)
Jerusalem Bible (1966)
New English Bible with the Apocrypha (1970)
New American Bible (1970)
Revised Standard Version, an Ecumenical Edition (1973)
Good News Bible / Today's English Version (1976)
New International Version (1978)
New Jerusalem Bible (1987)
Revised English Bible (1989)
New Revised Standard Version (1990)
Contemporary English Version (1995)
Contemporary English Version Global (2005)
Common English Bible (2011)

Additional question: Which Bible version do you find most comfortable to read?

Sacraments

What are sacraments?

We are a sacramental people. We are not simply hearers of the Word—
as important as that is—but we are also about touch and sight and smell
and taste. And this is where sacraments come in, visible and tangible
signs of invisible but very real grace. Through the stuff of life—water,
oil, bread, wine—we encounter the grace of God afresh. As important
it is to hear and respond to the sacred stories in the Bible, we also find
initiation and inclusion, strength and renewal, hope and comfort in
the sacramental rites outlined in the Book of Common Prayer.

These rites point to a larger reality for us as Christians in the Episcopal tradition, a sacramental approach to life itself. Far from being
some modern innovation, this approach is grounded in the incarnation itself, rooted in the life, death, and resurrection of Jesus Christ.
In our creeds we profess that in Jesus, God was incarnate. The infant
Jesus was not simply wrapped in swaddling cloths; he was clothed in
flesh and blood. The Divine became truly human. As he grew to adulthood, Jesus was able to heal people's infirmities with just a word, and
yet how often he chose to do more: touch the "unclean" leper who had
not been touched in Wholeness and healing, not just of the body but
also of the soul, comes not simply from hearing a word spoken, but
also from touch and taste.

Baptism and Eucharist are known as sacraments of the gospel,
having their origins in the life and ministry of Jesus. The Prayer Book
also recognizes five other sacramental rites that "evolved in the Church
under the guidance of the Holy Spirit."[1] These include confirmation,

---

1. Book of Common Prayer, 860.

ordination, holy matrimony, reconciliation of a penitent, and unction, or the blessing with oil of the sick and dying.

The sacraments are ongoing reminders of God's incarnational presence. We are immersed in them through our services, our rites and rituals. And so we can, like spiritual detectives, look for the footprints and fingerprints of God in all kinds of places and people. We can point to where God encounters us anew through the stuff of life. More than this, at the end of each Eucharist we are reminded that we, in turn, are called to be God's sacraments to the world about us— visible, tangible signs of divine grace. We who are the baptized followers of Christ are to be, as one saint once wisely put it, the hands and feet of God in our world.

Additional question: How have you encountered God in "the stuff of life"?

Why is Baptism so important?

One of the most powerful professions in the entire Prayer Book is found not in the main part of a service itself, but rather in the rubrics, those italicized instructions before the services that are meant to elucidate how things are to be done. On page 298, in the rubrics for the baptismal service, Baptism is described as "full initiation by water and the Holy Spirit into Christ's Body the Church."

To understand how it comes to be the Christian rite of initiation, we must go back to our roots in ancient Judaism. The very word "baptism" literally means "washing," and at the time of Christ, a ceremonial washing with water was known as Mikveh (or Mikvah). Mikveh was used for Jews in need of ritual purification following some kind of defilement, so that they could be cleansed and thereby allowed to participate in the Temple. The ritual washing also was part of the initiation rite for Gentiles wishing to convert to the Jewish faith. As noted in the Gospels, John the Baptist offered a "baptism of repentance" in the River Jordan to any penitents who sought a fresh start, a new life. Jesus was one of many who came to John to be baptized, though John, showing awareness of Jesus' identity as one who would "baptize in the Holy Spirit and in fire," was reluctant to baptize him. Jesus insisted and, as he came up out of the water, a heavenly voice proclaimed him to be God's Beloved, "with you I am well pleased" (Luke 3:16, 22). For Jesus, this act marked the beginning of his public ministry.

Even so, from the very beginning of the church, Christian Baptism has been about purification, conversion, and the call to ministry. In the Acts of the Apostles, on the day of Pentecost Peter called on a crowd of thousands to "repent, and be baptized every one of you in the name of Jesus Christ so that your sins may be forgiven; and you will receive the gift of the Holy Spirit" (2:38). Throughout the centuries there have been significant differences among the various Christian groups on how Baptism is to be administered. Some practice total immersion, either outside in a river or stream, or indoors in some kind of a tub or pool. Others either pour or sprinkle water over the head, usually over a baptismal font. In the end, however, Baptism is all about new life. As the Prayer Book attests, through it we are "cleansed from sin and born again."

Additional question: Why is washing such an apt symbol of new life?

Why do Episcopalians practice infant Baptism?

More than the baptismal process, there also have been through the years different convictions among churches about who can be baptized. To this day, many Christian churches will baptize only adults, noting that persons need to be of sufficient age to understand what they are doing and must make a personal profession of faith in Jesus Christ in order to be baptized. This is also known as "Believer's Baptism."

Episcopalians, however, are among those who also baptize infants and young children. The idea of this goes back to the church's earliest days, as in the Acts of the Apostles when it speaks of "the entire household" being included in the new life. Some second- and third-century Christian texts make reference to the baptizing of infants, with the so-called Apostolic Tradition of Hippolytus noting that parents make promises on the children's behalf. This practice continues today in the Episcopal Prayer Book service. Parents and godparents—those chosen sponsors who show an interest in the child's personal development and, implicitly, spiritual growth—agree to be responsible for seeing that the child "is brought up in the Christian faith and life," and that by their "prayers and witness" they will help the child to grow "into the full stature of Christ."

While critics of infant baptism might speak of the inability of the child to make his or her own promises, the rite's proponents instead point out that Baptism is first and foremost about what God does, not what we say or do. Just as a baby has no choice about being physically born or adopted into a family, but hopefully will grow into an awareness of what it means to be part of that family, even so in Baptism the child is "sealed by the Holy Spirit . . . and marked as Christ's own for ever." This is by God's grace, not because of anything he or she has done. The Prayer Book further asserts, "The bond which God establishes in Holy Baptism is indissoluble."[2] Amidst the many changes and chances of this life that come our way, we can take comfort in the fact that we are beloved by God, not just for a moment but forever, and that the bonds that connect us to our Creator and Redeemer do not dissolve. Baptism is the visible sign of that wondrous grace!

Additional question: Have you witnessed a Baptism? What did it mean to you?

What do Episcopalians think about private confession?

It is interesting that Thomas Cranmer, the English reformer who gave us the Book of Common Prayer, initially acknowledged not two, but three key sacraments: Baptism, Eucharist, and Penance, recognizing the importance of confessing one's sins before God. But Cranmer's Prayer Book eventually grounded this penitential emphasis in group worship, with the entire congregation participating in public confession of sins in the Eucharist as well as in Morning and Evening Prayer. Such corporate repentance was not limited to a single part of the Eucharistic service either, but found its way into several places in the service, including the "Prayer of Humble Access" immediately before receiving Communion: "We do not presume to come to this thy Table, merciful Lord, trusting in our own righteousness. . . . We are not worthy so much as to gather up the crumbs under thy table."[3]

Although this is the form of confession experienced by most Episcopalians, the fact is that we do still retain private confession as well. In the Prayer Book, there is a service called "Reconciliation of a Penitent," which provides two forms of a service for those wanting to unburden themselves of serious sins in private conversation with a priest, and receive absolution. As in the Roman Catholic service of

---

2. Book of Common Prayer, 298.

3. Book of Common Prayer, 337.

Penance, the Episcopal priest is morally bound to honor the confidence of the penitent and not reveal the contents of the confession. In a poignant moment of connection following the absolution, the priest declares, "Go in peace, and pray for me, a sinner."

For many Christians in the twenty-first century, private confession may feel unfamiliar and even awkward. Yet we have become quite comfortable with therapy and counseling, understanding how important it is to be free from things that are unhealthy for us. Confession complements this, while acknowledging that our selfish words, actions, and thoughts actually have repercussions for our relationships with God and others. Jesus brought peace and healing when he pronounced, "Your sins are forgiven." Such absolution can make one whole. Private confession may not be required for Episcopalians, but it can be a powerful spiritual tool, a sacramental rite that makes a difference in one's life. This is why we have an unofficial rule about private confession: "All may, some should, none must."

Additional question: Why say "some should" in regards to private confession?

What is the point of confirmation?

For many years, confirmation was a kind of second part to Baptism, a necessary next step in the Christian initiation process and a requirement before one could receive Holy Communion. Like a bar mitzvah, confirmation was also a coming-of-age ritual, usually experienced around age twelve. All this changed with the 1979 version of the Prayer Book. With the assertion that Holy Baptism was "full initiation by water and the Holy Spirit into Christ's Body the Church," it seemed to some as if the purpose for confirmation no longer existed. For others, however, it was a wonderful opportunity for the rite to evolve from a coming-of-age ritual to an adult reaffirmation of one's baptismal vows, a way of publicly saying "Yes" to God, an "altar call," as it were. As the introductory rubrics for the confirmation service in the 1979 Prayer Book make clear: "In the course of their Christian development, those baptized at an early age are expected, when they are ready and have been duly prepared, to make a mature public affirmation of their faith and commitment to the responsibilities of their Baptism."[4]

---

4. Book of Common Prayer, 412.

In the service, sometimes held at the diocesan cathedral with candidates from many congregations present, the confirmands all reaffirm their renunciation of evil and renew their commitment to Jesus Christ as Savior and Lord. The rest of the congregation present also makes a promise to "do all in [their] power to support these persons in their life in Christ." The bishop, as the visible representation of the church universal, then lays hands upon each confirmand, saying, "Strengthen, O Lord, your servant with your Holy Spirit, empower him/her for your service, and sustain him/her all the days of his/her life."[5] Those who have already been confirmed in another similar tradition, such as Roman Catholic or Eastern Orthodox, are instead "recognized" by the bishop as members of the "one holy catholic and apostolic Church" and "received in the fellowship of this Communion." Whether one is confirmed or received, this is no rebaptizing, but rather a call to mission and ministry as mature followers of Christ, recalling the Great Commission, when Jesus called his companions to go and "make disciples," not simply add new members to the rolls.

Additional question: Why is a public adult profession of faith important?

Who is allowed to receive Communion in the Episcopal Church?

As noted already, at one time it was necessary for someone to be confirmed before being allowed to receive Communion, thereby precluding children under the age of twelve. With the affirmation in the 1979 Prayer Book that Baptism alone is the sacramental rite of initiation, Communion became available to Episcopalians of all ages. This was a fairly dramatic and difficult change for those who believed that communicants should be of an "age of understanding" before being allowed to receive. If, however, Baptism indeed marks new birth, the adoption of one into the family, then it follows that the "family meal" is open to all members of the family, even the youngest.

As for an "age of understanding," a quick review of church history will reveal that both wars and wars of words have been fought by adults who disagreed about the nature and meaning of Communion. How often have clergy, parents, and other adults spoken with awe of

---

5. Book of Common Prayer, 418.

the moment when a young child's hands open in eager anticipation of receiving the body of Christ. No, they may not be able to explain transubstantiation, consubstantiation, or real presence, but then many adults cannot do so either. But they are all part of the family, whatever their age. True, there are some Episcopal congregations that prepare children for their "First Communion," but this is a matter of local custom.

Similarly, our Church welcomes not only our own, but Christians from other traditions and denominations, to receive Communion. This is in contrast with the Roman Catholic Church, where what is sometimes called "closed Communion" is the norm, meaning that only Catholics in good standing may receive the consecrated bread and wine. Because Episcopalians understand Baptism to be "full initiation into Christ's Body the Church," not simply into the Episcopal Church, we welcome and happily invite all who are baptized and are accustomed to receiving Communion in their tradition to join us at the Holy Table.

As for persons of other faiths, or those who for whatever reason cannot receive Communion, they are still most welcome to come to the altar rail and receive a blessing from the priest, thereby honoring their presence and reminding them that they too are beloved by God and esteemed guests at the family meal.

Additional question: What is your most meaningful memory of receiving Communion?

What are the other sacramental rites and pastoral services and why do they matter?

Although Episcopalians give special recognition of the two "sacraments of the gospel," Baptism and the Eucharist or Holy Communion, the Prayer Book also includes services for the other sacramental rites, which all together take us through the life journey from birth to death. Besides confirmation and reconciliation of a penitent, these include matrimony or marriage, holy orders or ordination, and unction or the blessing of the sick and dying. Added to these in the Prayer Book are services marking important pastoral moments, such as the thanksgiving for the birth or adoption of a child and the burial of the dead. And beyond the Prayer Book, there is a collection approved and amended by each meeting of the General Convention called *The Book of Occasional Services.* This supplemental text includes special seasonal liturgies, as well as pastoral services such as the celebration of a home, the blessing of a pregnant woman, and the anniversary of a marriage.

Not all Episcopal congregations make full use of the richness of our sacramental and pastoral tradition, but for those who do, there is much that is gained. The purpose of all these sacramental rites and pastoral services, after all, is to remind us that our lives are marked by the presence of God and inclusion in a community of faith and love. In good times and in hard times, God is always present and ready to offer us blessing. And the congregation is with us as a tribe or extended family to share in the ups and downs we experience.

When a child is born to a member of the church, all are reminded in the service that this is "a joyous and solemn occasion in the life of a family and also an occasion for rejoicing in the Christian community." When two persons come together in Holy Matrimony, the entire congregation is asked, "Will all of you witnessing these promises do all in your power to uphold these two persons in their marriage?" And when it is time to bid a loved one farewell, the congregation offers thanks to God "for giving him to us, his family and friends, to know and to love as a companion on our earthly pilgrimage."[6] The sacraments and pastoral services are our road markers along the way, reminding us that we are never alone. God is present in every significant moment, and our fellow Episcopalians are present with us as well.

Additional question: What is the most memorable service you have experienced?

---

6. Book of Common Prayer, 493.

Book of Common Prayer

How was the Prayer Book formed?

The Book of Common Prayer was born during the days of the Reformation when the Church of England separated from the Church of Rome. The archbishop of Canterbury under Henry VIII, Thomas Cranmer, replaced the multitude of books and materials that previously had been required by clergy to lead services with a single volume that could be easily carried, read, and understood by clergy and lay members alike. The result was the 1549 Book of Common Prayer, a remarkable and groundbreaking work that was in English, not Latin, reflecting his desire that the services of the church be in a language "understanded (sic) by the people." In his preface to that original edition, Cranmer claimed that, because of its clarity and ease of use, English clergy and laity would "need nothing for their public service, but this book and the Bible."[1]

That original Prayer Book and, even more so, Cranmer's revision in 1552 reveal the strong Protestant influence on Cranmer's thinking. While he ensured that England would retain Catholic sacramental practice as well as the traditional orders of bishops and priests, his Prayer Book dispensed with many of the accouterments and medieval excesses that had been added on through the centuries. Cranmer also honored the strong monastic tradition in England by giving weight to the services of Morning and Evening Prayer (Matins and Vespers), which actually displaced the Eucharist as the primary services on Sunday. Two more English revisions followed, with the 1662 book, a reflection of the later Elizabethan age, remaining the official Prayer Book to this day.

---

1. Book of Common Prayer, 867.

The heritage of revision, however, has continued in England. After twenty years experimentation with the Alternative Service Book, a new twenty-first-century creation entitled Common Worship was authorized to complement the 1662 Prayer Book, not supplant it. Common Worship is actually "a series of volumes which aims to provide a wide variety of prayers and liturgical resources for use within a common framework and common structures."[2] Thus, from its origins to today, we see the Prayer Book not only as a symbol of unity and communion, but also as a tool that represents both continuity and adaptation.

Additional question: Why is it important to use understandable language in worship?

Why are there different versions of the Prayer Book in different countries?

Following the American Revolution, the Church of England in the former colonies evolved into what would be called the Protestant Episcopal Church in the United States of America. The change in name was accompanied by necessary and obvious changes that helped "Americanize" our Prayer Book, including prayers for the president and the Congress in place of the traditional petitions for the English monarch. But the framers of the American book also recognized the opportunity before them to consider other, less apparent modifications. As they said in the preface to that 1789 Prayer Book, they welcomed "the happy occasion which was offered to them . . . to take a further review of the Public Service, and to establish such other alterations and amendments therein as might be deemed expedient."[3] In their work, they carefully walked the fine line of honoring the heritage they had received from the Church of England and addressing the needs of "local circumstance."

Like its English counterpart, the American book has gone through three subsequent revisions, each in turn authorized by the General Convention of the Episcopal Church, our highest legislative body. The 1979 Prayer Book remains the version still in use today, supplemented by additional resources such as the *Alternative Service Book*, *Enriching Our Worship*, and *Holy Women, Holy Men*.

---

2. Common Worship (London: Church House Publishing, 2000), preface.

3. Book of Common Prayer, 11.

As the years went by and other British colonies gained independence from the mother country, their churches in turn adapted the Prayer Book to meet their respective languages and cultural contexts. As it says in the preface to the New Zealand Prayer Book, it is important that it had been "created in our own Pacific cultural setting, and shaped by our own scholarship. It belongs to our environment and our people."[4] Some churches in the Anglican Communion who have developed an entirely new Prayer Book have created Eucharistic services and Morning and Evening Prayer in their own languages, honoring the past while meeting the needs of the present. In all these situations, the introduction to the New Zealand book says it best when it notes that "the purpose of liturgy is not to protect particular linguistic forms. It is to enable a community to pray."[5]

Additional question: What "local circumstances" could you or your parish address?

Why is the Prayer Book so important to Episcopalians?

The Book of Common Prayer is both our tangible sign of unity and our treasure chest. Other Christian groups breaking away from the Roman Catholic Church during the Reformation measured their unity by common agreement on various issues. Anglicans, on the other hand, instead pointed to worship—common prayer—as the basis for togetherness. At its best, this has meant that we can argue and debate any number of things, but still pick up our Prayer Books and come to worship as one body. In this way, it is both a symbol of, and a tool for, bridge-building in the midst of differences.

Related to this, the Prayer Book offers assurance to church members traveling away from home that we can enter any Episcopal church and find a sense of familiarity. It does not matter if this other church has a different look, or different styles of music, or different types of clergy, or parishioners who have different ideas about any number of things. Even if there are no actual books in the pews—or no pews!—but instead overhead projectors and screens, or prepared worship programs, we can still hear and repeat familiar words from that wonderfully familiar book. This is no small thing. Like the equally

---

4. New Zealand Prayer Book (London: Harper One, 1989), ix.

5. New Zealand Prayer Book, xiii.

familiar signs bearing an Episcopal shield and the words, "The Episcopal Church Welcomes You," we can be fairly certain that the church we then enter, for all its differences, will still be a spiritual home away from home. This is the practical power of the Prayer Book.

Having said all this, there is another dimension to the Prayer Book that, sadly, is often overlooked by many Episcopalians who never open its pages between Sunday services. It is quite common for the Prayer Books in church pews to have the small section devoted to the Eucharist worn and even shabby, while the rest of the pages appear untouched, practically new. This makes sense, given the fact that the Eucharist is the principle service of the Church. But if we do even basic exploration, we will discover that between its covers there exists a wealth of resources not only for public worship but also for private prayer, study, and spirituality. It is a gift for us and also for each of us.

Additional question: How could you make better use of your Prayer Book?

How does the liturgy work in a typical service of Holy Eucharist?

The word "liturgy" means the "work of the people" and a public duty. The service is not intended to be a concert, where you sit back and simply enjoy a beautiful choir. Instead, it is an opportunity for the people of God to come together and recognize in God who God is (this is the literal meaning of giving God due worth—hence "worth-ship") and to find in their worship the call to serve the world.

There are many different forms for the liturgy of the Holy Eucharist. This answer will focus on what we call Rite II, which is probably the form that is most often used.

The service starts with a recognition of the season in the church calendar we are observing. From Advent (four weeks before Christmas) through Easter and beyond, we tell every year, through the church calendar, the story of our faith. Advent is the season of preparation (both for the first coming of Christ, but also for the second); Christmas is the moment when we receive the incredible truth that God became a vulnerable baby, dependent (almost certainly) on a teenage mother; Epiphany is when we recognize how the light of Christ is available to the whole world; Lent is the start of the journey into adulthood and reaches a climax in the tragedy of Good Friday;

and Easter is the moment of celebration and conquest over the trag-edy of sin and suffering. The colors in the Church change as we move through the seasons. And we focus on different aspects of discipleship as we move through the different seasons—so in Lent the focus is repentance, while in Christmas, the stress is gratitude.

Next we move to the "Word" part of the service. This is the sec-tion where we learn about who God is. Christians believe God has told us (revealed to us) who God is. We learn through the Written Word (the Bible), the Eternal Word (in Christ), and the Proclaimed Word (through the preacher). Having discovered that God is good, loving, merciful, and eager to be in relationship with each and every one of us, we then move to the section of the service where we enjoy the privilege of prayer.

As we pray, we bring our petitions for the world in which we live and our own concerns. We believe that God is interested in both the big and the small. So we pray for those parts of the world that are hurt-ing and, at the same time, bring our worries about relationships and money. Normally, we conclude the prayers with confession.

In some Christian traditions, there is an emphasis on that crucial moment when you turn to Jesus to be forgiven. In the Episcopal tra-dition, we tend to find that we need that moment every single week. Faith is a journey. We know that we have many rough edges that need divine attention. So we confess weekly, hoping and trusting that others can see the gradual progress toward a life less egocentric and more other-centric.

Liturgically, the halfway point of the service is the peace. This is rich in symbolism. It comes just before the offertory. So we are reminded of our Lord's instruction in the Sermon on the Mount (Mat-thew 5) that before we make an offering to God, we should ensure that we are at peace with our brother. So this is the moment, when we sym-bolically reach out to all those we find difficult. In the moment of the handshake, we are not simply recognizing the person in front of us as a person with whom we strive to be at peace, but we also reach out to the person who is driving us crazy at work. In addition, we also reach out to the person who hurt us in our past. It is amazing the number of people who are damaging others because they were damaged by a failed relationship or a parent who neglected them. In the Peace, we invite the peace of the Lord to heal that pain. We strive to be at peace with all those in the present and past who have hurt us.

The rest of the service is dominated by the Great Thanksgiving and the communion of the people. This is the long prayer led by the priest on behalf of the congregation. Learning to be grateful is a vital part of discipleship. It is a great privilege to have the gift of life—so we should be thankful; it is a great privilege to have family and friends—so we should be thankful; it is a great privilege to see, hear, touch, and taste—so we should be thankful; it is a great privilege to enjoy beautiful music and fine art—so we should be thankful—and so the list goes on. In the Great Thanksgiving, we give thanks to God the Father for all this, but we also give thanks to God for the tragic.

The ultimate tragedy that we thank God for is the tragedy of a young man killed by an occupying power some 2,000 years ago. For it is in that life and tragic death, we believe that the redemption of the world is made possible. As we reflect on this life-giving tragedy, so we find ourselves reflecting on the tragic in our own lives.

The tragic haunts every human life. Learning to handle the tragic is an important part of the Great Thanksgiving. As we handle the loss of a relative or the failed ambition, we have to learn to find "grace" in that tragedy. The gospel claim is that grace is embedded in the hardest of times. It is in the Great Thanksgiving that we invite God to show us where the grace is to be found. Sometimes it is impossible to see, but somewhere there will be grace.

After we have received the Eucharist, we are then ready for the postcommunion prayer. The purpose of the service is not ultimately to make us "feel good," but to equip us for work in the world. There is a hurting world outside the church building, which needs the good news of Christ. In the postcommunion prayer, we are sent out ready to advance the kingdom of God.

From football to Beethoven, appreciation takes time. This is also true of liturgy. There is a skill set to learn. Initially, it can be frustrating. There are too many books; and there will be moments when you are not sure exactly where you are in the Book of Common Prayer. But slowly, over the weeks, the patterns will become clear. And slowly, over the weeks, God will work on your life so you too can be a vehicle of the love of Christ to the world.

Additional question: Do you have questions about this or that detail in the liturgy? Identify those questions and find an experienced Episcopalian friend to help you understand the experience so much more.

What is the relationship between the Bible and the Prayer Book?

It has been said that 70 percent of the Prayer Book is taken directly from the Holy Scriptures. With whole passages, quotations, and allusions included—not to mention the entire Psalter—the Prayer Book truly is a biblical book.

Just consider the Eucharistic service. It has the option of opening with the Decalogue, or Ten Commandments, straight out of the book of Exodus, or penitential sentences from Mark's Gospel, the First Letter of John, and Hebrews. The Gloria is born out of the angels' song at the birth of Jesus in Luke's Gospel, and the Kyrie (Lord, have mercy) is a plea found on the lips of different supplicants seeking healing from Jesus in the Gospels. The Collect of the Day ties in with the Lessons, which are taken directly from the Old Testament, the Psalms, the New Testament Epistles, and the Gospels, utilizing the lectionary at the back of the Prayer Book to determine which readings are to be used on particular days. The sermon, now as in centuries past, is an exposition of one or more of the readings for the day. The creed, dating back to the fourth-century Council of Nicaea, is a systematic recitation of what we believe about God, all grounded in Holy Scripture. The Prayers of the People and the Confession, while not direct quotations, are clearly grounded in biblical language and thought. And the Peace is taken directly from Paul's letters. The Eucharistic Prayer has at its heart the words of Jesus from the Last Supper, and the Lord's Prayer is lifted directly from the pages of the Gospels. All this Scripture, and just in one small section of the Prayer Book!

Looking at the rest of the Prayer Book, individual Episcopalians can begin and end their days with biblically based devotional aids in the form of the Daily Office and the Daily Office lectionary, reading through the Bible in a two-year period. The Catechism and Historical Documents offer study tools. The other pastoral services and additional prayers are filled with Scripture. And, as noted, the inclusion of the entire Psalter allows us individually or in groups to pray, sing, or chant the Psalms, the Bible's original "hymnal." There is no doubt: with such focused biblical resources together in one volume, the Prayer Book is a powerful spiritual tool.

Additional question: Why is it important that the Prayer Book is biblically grounded?

How is the current Prayer Book arranged?

The 1979 Book of Common Prayer, the version still in use in the Episcopal Church today, represents a significant departure in style and
content from its predecessors, a result of decades of intense liturgical
research and discovery, while at the same time including much of what
has come before. It opens with the church calendar, displaying the days
dedicated to the commemoration of various saints.

Note that with the Daily Office and the Eucharist, as well as the
collects (the prayers that collect the themes of the readings for the day),
there is a Rite I and a Rite II version of the same or similar content.
Rite I uses Elizabethan English, with "thee" and "hast" and "it is meet
and right so to do" while Rite II uses modern English. Other more
subtle differences reflect the more penitential nature of the old rite,
with certain prayers included—"we do not presume to come to this
thy table"—that are not found in the Rite II. The inclusion of Rite I is
recognition of the importance of Thomas Cranmer's original language
and intent with the first Prayer Book centuries ago. Some congregations still prefer it to the contemporary version.

Then come liturgies for special feasts or fasts of the Church,
such as Ash Wednesday and Easter Vigil, which, in turn, are followed by the services of Holy Baptism and the Eucharist. Baptism is
recognized as THE initiatory rite of the Church, by which we come
fully into the family of Christ. All other rites, responsibilities, and
privileges flow from this. There follow the "Pastoral Offices," those
other sacramental rites and services used regularly in a congregation,
such as the marriage service or burials. Note that additional services
used less regularly can be found in a supplemental volume, *The Book
of Occasional Services.*

The "Episcopal Offices," which follow, are those that require a
bishop to officiate, including ordinations and consecrations of church
buildings. These are trailed by the Psalter, other prayers and thanks-
givings, the catechism (a wonderful teaching tool), and "historical
documents," which include ancient statements of faith. Rounding out
the Prayer Book are the lectionaries for the Eucharistic services and
daily devotions. The book's clear organization makes it a valuable tool
to be used.

Additional question: What sections of the Prayer Book do you
need to explore?

What is the lectionary, and how is it used in worship services and private study?

While in several other Christian churches, it is the preacher who chooses the biblical passage on which she or he will then preach, in so-called liturgical churches, including the Episcopal Church, the various Scripture readings actually come from the lectionary and the preacher (and congregation) has to live with whatever is assigned for that day.

The lectionary we use today is a three-year cycle of preassigned biblical passages that are read each week in our worship services. The tradition for this can be traced back to early Judaism, as certain readings were preselected for specific feasts or holy days. By the time of the Middle Ages, Jewish and Christian faith groups alike were using lectionaries in their services. While one such lectionary is found in the back of our Prayer Book, in more recent years the Episcopal Church has joined other Christian denominations in using the Revised Common Lectionary, which itself has drawn from the post-Vatican II Roman Catholic lectionary. In the three-year cycle, the first year focuses on Matthew's Gospel, the second on Mark's Gospel, and the third on Luke's Gospel, while the Gospel of John is woven into the Easter season. Readings from the Old Testament, the Hebrew Scriptures, are tied into the Gospel reading for the day, and the New Testament selection from the epistles, or letters, are read in an ongoing cycle. The Psalms, which are printed in their entirety in the Prayer Book, are read, chanted, or sung in unison, responsively, or antiphonally between the Old Testament and New Testament readings.

We also have in the back of Book of Common Prayer a two-year Daily Office lectionary that can allow individual Episcopalians to read through the entire Bible in two years. This lectionary is more unabridged than the one used during services and contains many of the difficult passages otherwise not heard on a Sunday. It can serve as a vital part of an individual's daily discipline of prayer and reflection, either using it in conjunction with the offices of Morning Prayer and Evening Prayer as found in the front of the Prayer Book (along with Noon Prayers and the end-of-day Compline service), or simply in personal prayer.

Additional question: What parts of the Bible have you not yet read, and why not?

What is *The Book of Occasional Services* and how does it relate to the Prayer Book?

Since the creation of the 1979 Book of Common Prayer, it has been clear that there is a need from time to time for additional services to be made available to Episcopal congregations. But this did not have to mean that a new revision of the Prayer Book would be required. After all, the *Hymnal 1982* has been joined in subsequent years by several supplemental hymn books, including *Lift Every Voice* and *Sing* I and II; *Wonder, Love, and Praise*; *Voices Found*; and *My Heart Sings Out*. For this reason, other books and booklets have been authorized by General Convention for use in worship, to supplement the Prayer Book, not to replace or revise it. These include *The Book of Occasional Services, Lesser Feasts and Fasts, Enriching Our Worship,* and, most recently, *Holy Women, Holy Men.* All are available through Church Publishing Incorporated, a division of the Church Pension Group that provides liturgical as well as other printed and online resources for the Episcopal Church.

The Book of Occasional Services is just what its title declares it to be, a compilation of services that are only occasionally used or, as its preface states, "do not occur with sufficient frequency to warrant their inclusion"[6] in the Prayer Book. The book is divided into sections, the first of which concerns congregational services for the various liturgical seasons. Hence it includes seasonal blessings, prayers for the lighting of the Advent wreath, notes on the foot washing and stripping of the altar on Maundy Thursday, and lesser known services such as Tenebrae and the Candlemas Procession. This section is followed by a collection of pastoral services, including the welcoming of new people to the congregation, the celebration of a home, and preparation materials for adults who will be baptized, as well as the commissioning of lay ministries in the Church or a public healing service. The Standing Commission on Liturgy and Music has the responsibility of presenting for possible inclusion those liturgies and resources that are then voted on by General Convention. As the book evolves with the inclusion of new materials or the amending of others, each new edition bears on its cover the date of the General Convention that authorized it.

Additional question: What liturgical resources would you find most meaningful?

---

6. The Book of Occasional Services, (New York: Church Publishing 1994), 7.

What about *Enriching Our Worship* and *Holy Women, Holy Men?*

Enriching Our Worship, published right before the turn of the new century, is not about additional services but rather about alternative forms of Prayer Book services, "to expand the language, images, and metaphors used in worship," as it says in its preface. The expansive language includes recovery of ancient biblical and patristic images, such as the identification of Christ with Wisdom, in order to speak of God in ways that are not just the familiar masculine imagery so long used. "Expanding our vocabulary of prayer and the ways in which we name the Holy One bear witness to the fact that the mystery of God transcends all categories of knowing, including those of masculine and feminine."[7]

The "book" is actually five small volumes, the first dealing with the Daily Office, the Great Litany, and the Eucharist; the second with Ministry with the Sick and Dying, and Burial of a Child; the third with Burial Rites for Adults; the fourth with the Renewal of Ministry, and the Welcoming of a New Rector or Pastor; and the fifth with Liturgies Related to Childbearing, Childbirth, and Loss. All of the resources included under the umbrella of *Enriching Our Worship* are to be used under the direction of the diocesan bishop, thereby connecting the congregations with the chief liturgical officer of the diocese.

Holy Women, Holy Men: Celebrating the Saints follows the tradition of *Lesser Feasts and Fasts* in focusing on those special heroes of the faith who are to be honored on different days in the Church's calendar. Quoting John Mason Neale's great hymn that opens the recent volume, "Worthy deeds they wrought, and wonders, worthy of the Name they bore; we, with meetest praise and sweetest, honor them for evermore." The collection includes short biographies of each saint, along with prayers or collects for their feast day's service, as well as suggested biblical readings for that day. The book's goal, as expressed in its preface is to "give increased expression to the many and diverse ways in which Christ, through the agency of the Holy Spirit, has been present in the lives of men and women across the ages, just as Christ continues to be present in our own day."[8]

Additional question: Which heroes of the faith personally mean the most to you?

---

7. Enriching Our Worship (New York: Church Publishing 1998), v.

8. *Holy Women, Holy Men* (New York: Church Publishing 2010), 7.

The Church

How did the Episcopal Church come to be?

We hear in the preface of the 1789 American Prayer Book echoes of the Declaration of Independence: "But when in the course of Divine Providence, these American States became independent with respect to civil government, their ecclesiastical independence was necessarily included." What this meant for the Church of England in the States was its evolution into a church that would, in the words of William White, first presiding bishop, "contain the constituent principles of the Church of England and yet be independent of foreign jurisdiction of influence."[1] White himself understood something about the importance of balancing continuity with change, having earlier served as chaplain to the Continental Congress. He had eaten and talked with Adams, Jefferson, and Rush. He appreciated the need to create structures that made sense, that offered checks and balances in governance, that allowed for a greater number of voices in the decision-making process.

The result was the Protestant Episcopal Church in the United States of America. The appellation "Protestant" was clearly chosen to distinguish it from the Roman Catholic Church, the other liturgically focused church in the new nation. Far more interesting was the word "Episcopal." Derived from the Greek term *episkopos*, it literally means "bishop." Ours is a church of bishops. In fact, in the back of *The Episcopal Church Annual* is found a list of all the bishops who have been ordained and consecrated to that office in this Church.

The first of these is not William White, but rather Samuel Seabury, who had to go to Scotland to be made a bishop, since the

---

1. William White, *The Case of the Episcopal Churches in the United States Considered* (Philadelphia: David C. Claypoole, 1782).

Church of England would not yet acknowledge the validity of this new church. For this reason, the flag of the Episcopal Church would forever bear witness to both its "parents" by containing both the red-on-white cross of St. George (patron saint of England) and, in the top left corner, the white-on-blue cross of St. Andrew (patron saint of Scotland). The Church of England soon relented and ordained the next few American bishops, who in turn kept the succession going through the years.

Yet even with the emphasis on bishops in our system, from the beginning this church has welcomed and encouraged full participation in all levels of governance to clergy and to laity.

Additional question: What strikes you when you reflect on the origins of the Episcopal Church?

Why is the Church now referred to as TEC instead of ECUSA?

Although the Church was born and grounded in the American experience, it has grown beyond the borders of the United States. Today, for example, the Episcopal Church includes dioceses in American territories such as Puerto Rico, the Virgin Islands, Guam and Micronesia; in Caribbean nations such as Haiti, Honduras, and the Dominican Republic; in South American countries such as Colombia, Ecuador, and Venezuela; and in far-off lands such as Taiwan and the Convocation of Churches in Europe. Indeed, the largest diocese numerically in the Episcopal Church, though also one of the most challenged ones financially, is Haiti. Until recent years, other places were also included that have since become autonomous provinces in their own right with whom we have ongoing special covenant relationships, including Mexico, Brazil, Central America, the West African country of Liberia, and the Philippines. And we share with the churches in Canada and the West Indies in metropolitan oversight of the church in Cuba.

This expansion beyond the borders of the States has occurred gradually over time and until very recently has been largely ignored by American Episcopalians. Thus, for some time we were known by the acronym ECUSA, which stood for "Episcopal Church in the United States of America." This was, of course, virtually the same name as from the first days of independence from the Church of England, the only difference being the gradual dropping of the word "Protestant" to distinguish Episcopalians from other less liturgically focused churches. In the early twentieth century, the official name of the corporate organization became "The Domestic and Foreign Missionary Society of the Protestant Episcopal Church in the United States of America." While this appropriately recognized the nondomestic outposts of the Church, it still did so from within a missionary and sometimes colonialist model.

Today, although the corporate name remains for official purposes, the Church acknowledges its multinational character by using as its self-designation "The Episcopal Church" or TEC for short. And in both gatherings of the whole Church and documents for it, Spanish and French are increasingly and intentionally used alongside English. Still, there remains a great need for Episcopalians both within and outside the United States to learn more about and from one another.

Additional question: What are the benefits of being part of a multinational church?

How are decisions made in the Church?

From the earliest days of the Episcopal Church, lay people as well as clergy held significant roles of leadership. Not unlike the new nation with which it shared its origins, the American Church was grounded in its Constitution and Canons, or church laws, and governed through legislation enacted in a bicameral system. Meeting every three years, the General Convention of the Episcopal Church consists of the House of Deputies, which includes both lay and clerical leaders elected by their diocesan conventions, and the House of Bishops. In order for resolutions to be approved by General Convention, they must secure the necessary number of votes in both Houses.

The president of the House of Deputies, elected from within, oversees that House and makes deputy appointments to the commissions, committees, agencies, and boards (CCABs) that meet during the three-year interim between conventions. The presiding bishop, elected by the House of Bishops, presides over that House, and makes bishop appointments to the CCABs. In those three-year periods between conventions, a board known as the Executive Council serves as the decision-making body for the church.

Following a tradition that dates back to the early years of Christianity, the Episcopal Church is made up of 110 dioceses, or geographical units that in turn consist of congregations, chaplaincies, and other area ministries. Episcopalians recognize that, although we worship together on a local level, we are part of a larger whole. Dioceses are overseen by bishops who are supported in the work of oversight by standing committees of elected members both lay and ordained.

On the parish level, priests are chosen by their respective congregations, with the approval of the bishop. Vestries, consisting of lay members elected from within the parish, oversee the financial and temporal needs of the congregation, meeting regularly with the rector or vicar, the priest in charge of that parish.

It is little wonder that other parts of the Anglican Communion as well as some ecumenical partners are surprised when they learn of our polity, or governance, precisely because of how democratic and inclusive our structures are. To learn more about General Convention and Executive Council, go to *www.episcopalchurch.org* or *www.generalconvention.org*.

Additional question: How involved are you in your parish, diocese, or the larger Church?

What is the significance of the Baptismal Covenant for the Church?

In earlier ages, and even in some other churches today, lay persons have had little say in what would happen. This is decidedly not the case in the Episcopal Church! This is not only because of our history, but also because of the intentional grounding of every member's divine calling in the Baptismal Covenant. With the 1979 revision of the Book of Common Prayer, Holy Baptism—defined as "full initiation by water and the Holy Spirit into Christ's Body the Church"—was lifted up as THE foundation for all vocations, lay and ordained. It is an important part of every baptismal service, and is also used at other times throughout the church year, such as Easter, whenever there is a need for members to renew their commitment to God in Christ.

The Baptismal Covenant itself is a two-part question-and-answer interchange. First comes the Apostles' Creed, that ancient statement of faith in God as Creator, Redeemer, and life-giving Spirit. "Do you believe in God the Father? . . . Do you believe in Jesus Christ, the Son of God? . . . Do you believe in God the Holy Spirit?" Then follow five additional questions pertaining to the Christian life. "Will you continue in the apostles' teaching and fellowship, in the breaking of bread, and in the prayers? . . . Will you persevere in resisting evil, and, whenever you fall into sin, repent and return to the Lord? . . . Will you proclaim by word and example the Good News of God in Christ? . . . Will you seek and serve Christ in all persons, loving your neighbor as yourself? . . . Will you strive for justice and peace among all people, and respect the dignity of every human being?" To each of these questions, the respondents reply, "I will, with God's help" (BCP, 304–5).

What a marvelous reminder of who we are, and whose we are, "marked as Christ's own for ever." The Baptismal Covenant is about far more than simply giving intellectual assent to a set of academic propositions. No, it is about how we will choose to love God and our neighbor. For lay members, this is the great calling. If they take these promises seriously, then with God's help they can change lives and, ultimately, change the world. As for bishops, priests, and deacons, their ordination vows flow out of these essential promises made in Holy Baptism.

Additional question: What promise in the Baptismal Covenant resonates with you?

How do I become a member of the Episcopal Church?

We don't tend to stress membership in the Episcopal Church. It only really becomes an issue when the annual meeting arises. Instead, as we have already noted, we tend to stress the that anyone baptized with water in the name of the Holy Trinity is a part of the body of Christ and therefore a brother or a sister in Christ.

Technically, there are two ways you can become a member of the Episcopal Church. The first is through Baptism. When a person is baptized in the particular parish church, then technically that person is a member of that parish until they die or their records are transferred. Therefore, the second way you can become a member is by being "received" into the Episcopal Church or by being "transferred" from another Episcopal church. If you are a member of another Christian family, then you are received into the Episcopal Church; if you are a member of another Episcopal church, then your membership is simply transferred. The important feature is that you have been baptized.

Now given most of us get baptized as a baby, it is important to have ways of tracking commitment and involvement in a congregation.

There are three levels of involvement. The first is the communicant member; this is a person who at least takes Holy Communion three times a year. The second is a member in good standing. This means that you have been faithful in attending corporate worship and that you are involved in the congregational life (which includes making a pledge to give to support the life of the congregation). The third is a confirmed communicant member. Any baptized Christian can take the Eucharist in an Episcopal Church. However, once you reach maturity, you are expected to commit to the faith and reaffirm the work that God is doing in your life through baptism. This is known as confirmation.

One difficulty facing every major denomination is tracking its members. It is good when individuals take responsibility for their status within a congregation. We want people to join and get involved.

Additional question: Are you a member of an Episcopal church? If not, why not?

What are the roles of bishops, priests, and deacons in the Church?

All are called in Baptism to minister by word and action in Christ's name, but since the earliest days of the Church there have been some who have been set apart for special "ordained" ministries: namely, bishops, presbyters or priests, and deacons. The roles and duties of each are outlined in their respective ordinations services found near the end of the Prayer Book in a section called "episcopal services" because a bishop is required to lay hands on the individual and thereby ordain that person (or a minimum of three bishops in the case of a bishop). Ordained ministers in the Episcopal Church can trace their historic succession back to the earliest years of Christianity.

Besides having the authority to ordain, and thereby ensure that continuity of order, bishops also are known as the guardians of the faith and living symbols of the unity of the Church. The unique place of bishops in our system should not be underestimated. Without them, and the diocesan structure they oversee, we would be no more than individual congregations. By being part of a larger whole, and one that is marked by geography and not affinity of opinion, bishops' flocks are a sign to the world of the power of the gospel. Our communion is based not on agreement—as Jesus would say, even the Gentiles can do that!—but on grace and graciousness. As the Apostle Paul said in Galatians 3:28, "There is no longer Jew or Greek, there is no longer slave or free, there is no longer male nor female; for all of you are one in Christ Jesus." Bishops represent this unity and universality of the Church, which is why they alone can ordain, consecrate church buildings, and confirm or receive lay people.

Bishops, however, cannot personally oversee all the congregations that make up their diocesan flock, and so presbyters or priests serve as pastors and teachers on the local level. Like bishops, they can administer Baptism and preside at the Eucharist, hear confessions and marry and bury. They are both a part of their local congregation and apart from it, as they balance their work of comfort with that of challenge. They are pastors, yes, but they must at times also be prophets.

Deacons share in that prophetic role, and while they cannot preside at the Eucharist like bishops and priests, their special gift to the Church is to model servanthood and call all the people of God to greater service and engagement in their local communities and the world.

Additional question: Ask a bishop, priest, or deacon about his or her vocational call.

What is the Episcopal position on the ordination of women?

The question of ordaining women has been historically, and remains to this day, a controversial one. The argument of some Christian traditions is that Jesus only had male apostles, and therefore set the model for apostolic ministry ever since. Other traditions opposed to women's ordination point to New Testament texts such as 1 Timothy 2:11–15, which speaks of the need for women to keep silent and in submission, and further says that a woman is not permitted to have teaching authority over a man. To this day, the Roman Catholic Church does not permit women to be ordained as priests or bishops; neither do Orthodox Churches.

Anglicans are at very different points on the continuum on this issue. The first woman to be ordained a priest in the Anglican Communion was Li Tim-Oi in the diocese of Hong Kong and Macao in 1944. However, it would be decades before another woman was ordained. In the Episcopal Church, eleven women were made priests in July 1974.

Known thereafter as the "Philadelphia Eleven" (owing to the site of their ordination service), their orders were considered "irregular" until the General Convention of 1976 allowed for the ordination of women to all orders. It would, however, be over a decade before Barbara Harris was ordained and consecrated a bishop in the diocese of Massachusetts. Since then, the Anglican Churches of Aotearoa, New Zealand, and Polynesia, as well as Canada, Australia, and Southern Africa, have all ordained women as bishops, while Ireland and Scotland allow for it, but have had no such consecrations take place yet. The Church of England began ordaining women as priests in the early 1990s, and it looks like ordination to the episcopate will come in the next few years.

For those who support the ordination of women, the argument goes beyond a matter of justice and equal rights, though many will speak of this as well. But for many, this is also a gospel issue, a theological issue. For while it is true that the twelve apostles of Jesus were male, he also had a cadre of women, some named, who were key followers and financial supporters of his mission. Likewise, in Romans 16, Paul mentions as many women as men when he speaks of fellow leaders in his churches. And of course there is Mary Magdalene, who stayed at the foot of the cross when the apostles ran away and who was the first witness to the resurrection. From earliest days Mary was called "the apostle to the apostles," and was held in high esteem. It would be a few centuries later that she would be saddled with the stigma of being a prostitute, a claim with no scriptural basis.

Today, Episcopalians can find women in all orders of ordained ministry including, as of 2006, the presiding bishop of the Episcopal Church, Katharine Jefferts Schori, the first woman to serve as an Anglican Primate.

Additional question: How have you experienced women in ministerial leadership?

How do Episcopalians relate to other Christian churches?

In both the Baptismal Covenant and in the Nicene Creed recited at the Eucharist, Episcopalians affirm our standing in the "one, holy, catholic, and apostolic church." As such, the Episcopal Church recognizes the validity of other Christians' Baptism, regardless of their denominational tradition, as long as it was administered by water (the procedure—immersion, pouring, or sprinkling—is not important) and in the triune name of the Father, Son, and Holy Spirit. Similarly, Episcopalians welcome and encourage other baptized Christians to receive Communion in the service of Holy Eucharist. This is in contrast to the Roman Catholic Church, which only allows reception of Communion by practicing Roman Catholics. Episcopalians also formally "receive" Christians from other Christian traditions in which they previously had been confirmed by a bishop, rather than requiring a reconfirmation.

Perhaps it is because of our commitment to the larger whole that Episcopalians have been instrumental in the ecumenical movement on all levels—local, regional, national, and international. We remain active members and leaders in the National Council of Churches as well as the World Council of Churches, and are engaged in several bilateral dialogues with other Christian churches, such as the United Methodists and the Presbyterians. In recent years, we have been able to affirm "full communion" status with some churches, including the Evangelical Lutheran Church in America, the Northern and Southern Provinces of the Moravian Church in America, and the Old Catholic Church, among others. In practical terms, this means that our clergy can be fully interchangeable, i.e., an ELCA pastor can preside over the Eucharist in an Episcopal Church and vice versa.

Our standard for achieving full communion with another Christian body is a four-fold set of requirements ratified in the late nineteenth century by the General Convention meeting in Chicago and then honed further by the Lambeth Conference of Bishops, appropriately named the Chicago-Lambeth Quadrilateral. The requirements include belief in the Old and New Testaments as the written Word of God, recognition of Baptism and the Eucharist as the two sacraments of the gospel, affirmation of the Apostles' and Nicene Creeds, and acceptance of the historic succession of bishops.

Additional question: What have you learned from other non-Episcopal Christians?

How do Episcopalians relate to other religions?

Both on our own as well as in partnership with other Christian churches, Episcopalians have increasingly found ways to engage with other non-Christian religious groups. This has been particularly true with the other two Abrahamic faiths—Judaism and Islam—so called because they share with Christians a belief in one God (monotheism) that dates back to Abraham in the book of Genesis, "the father of faith."

While in past centuries our track record as Christians in interreligious relations has been remarkably poor—take note of the Crusades against the Muslims and the persecutions against Jews—in more recent times we have sought new ways to foster mutual understanding and cooperation. On both local and regional levels, shared prayer services, teaching opportunities, and joint community outreach projects have enabled Episcopalians to move beyond fear and misunderstanding into genuine cooperation. Although it is not permitted for non-Christians to partake of Holy Communion, many Episcopal congregations appropriately welcome members of other religions to come forward to the altar rail for a blessing.

On the larger level, official dialogues continue between the Episcopal Church and both Jewish and Islamic organizations, as well as other nonmonotheistic religious groups such as Hindus and Buddhists. The Cathedral Church of Sts. Peter and Paul in the diocese of Washington, more familiarly known as the Washington National Cathedral, often serves as a site of shared services in times of national crisis and celebration. The same is true of the Cathedral of St. John the Divine in New York City, Grace Cathedral in San Francisco, and countless other cathedrals and churches. Likewise, the presiding bishop of the Episcopal Church joins with other religious leaders in periodically issuing common statements on various social and political issues.

The same spirit of collaboration that marked the Episcopal Church's engagement in the ecumenical movement of the twentieth century seems to be growing in the interfaith arena. And in an increasingly global society, such efforts seem not only laudatory but necessary for the common good.

Additional question: What are some assumptions you have about other religions?

Anglican Communion

What is the Anglican Communion?

Although the Episcopal Church is relatively small in numbers compared to other Christian denominations in the United States, as part of the global fellowship that is the Anglican Communion, we are members of the third largest Christian group in the world, behind Roman Catholics and the Orthodox Church.

The New Zealand Prayer Book defines the Communion best in its catechism: "The Anglican Communion is a world-wide fellowship of self-governing churches holding the doctrine and ministry of the one, holy, catholic and apostolic church, and in communion with the Archbishop of Canterbury."[1] Because at first glance we look and sound like Roman Catholics, people will often mistake Anglicans for them, at times even joking that we are "Catholic-Lite." But note that while the Roman Catholic Church is a single global organization, with the pope the undisputed head over all parts, our Communion is a "fellowship" of churches that are national or regional and, quite significantly, "self-governing." It is the mix of autonomy and relationship that makes the Anglican Communion a unique manifestation of the body of Christ in the world. As famed Archbishop and Nobel Laureate Desmond Tutu once remarked, "We are messy, but very lovable."[2] We are together not by a top-down decree, but because of the recognition of our common life in Christ and our common heritage.

Historically, the Communion is natural outgrowth of the Church of England, spread to different parts of the globe with the expansion

1. New Zealand Book of Common Prayer, 962.

2. Desmond Tutu, as cited in Mike McCoy, "Going in Peace, or breaking in pieces? Anglican Unity and the Mission of God", *intermission,* volume 4, no.1 (February 1998): 32.

of British presence and influence. In Africa and Asia, Australia and New Zealand, and the Americas, it is possible to find an Anglican congregation. Again, the New Zealand Prayer Book succinctly encapsulates the Communion's evolution: "It initially grew from the historic faith of the English speaking peoples but is now present in many different cultures and languages."[3] As former colonies of the British Empire gained their independence, so too did their respective churches become autonomous provinces, while retaining the connection with the archbishop of Canterbury, one of the four "instruments of unity" for the Communion, along with the Lambeth Conference, the Anglican Consultative Council (which consists of elected representatives from all the provinces of the Communion, including bishops, clergy, and lay persons), and the Primates' Meeting.

Additional question: What does it mean to you to be part of a worldwide Communion?

Who is the archbishop of Canterbury and how do Episcopalians view him?

In the year 597, a monk named Augustine was sent by Pope Gregory I, often called "the Great," to the southeastern part of the British Isles, to bring the Christian gospel to the fair-skinned "angels," as Gregory called the local Anglo inhabitants. Landing in Kent, Augustine went to Canterbury and sought out the king of that land and was surprised to find that many, including King Ethelbert's wife, were already believers. Christianity had come to Britain in the earliest centuries of the faith, with two representatives from the Isles involved in the Council of Nicaea in 325, the council that gave us the Nicene Creed. What Augustine found, however, was different from the Roman tradition to which he was accustomed, with regional Celtic influences. After consulting with Gregory, Augustine took the best of what he found and the best of what he brought, and the Church in England was officially born, with Augustine himself appointed as its first archbishop.

One hundred and four men have succeeded him in that office, some achieving lasting fame, like Becket, martyred in Canterbury Cathedral for standing up to King Henry II, or Thomas Cranmer,

---

3. New Zealand Book of Common Prayer, 962.

Henry VIII's archbishop who initiated the Reformation in England, authored the Book of Common Prayer, and was killed at the order of Henry's daughter, Queen Mary. The archbishops of Canterbury have all served as bishops of their local diocese of Canterbury as well as chief primates of the Church in England, or the Church of England, as it became after the split with Rome during the Reformation. Since the late 1800s, archbishops have also served as focal points for the expanding fellowship of churches that is the Anglican Communion.

It is important to note that the archbishop of Canterbury is not an Anglican pope, but rather *primus inter pares*, "first among equals," a visible symbol and instrument of unity within the Communion. He serves as its chief spokesperson and ambassador, exerting influence over the Communion, but direct authority only over the Church of England itself (even that authority is shared with the archbishop of York, who oversees the northern province within England). As Episcopalians, we recognize the presiding bishop as the primate of this Church, but still show respect and affection for the archbishop of Canterbury as a living reminder of both our heritage and our ongoing relationship with the "Mother Church."

Additional question: Why is it significant to say that the archbishop is not our pope?

What is the Lambeth Conference of bishops and how did it come about?

As the Anglican Communion grew, so did its challenges. In the 1860s, bishops from different parts of the world, for different reasons, contacted the archbishop of Canterbury and requested a gathering of all bishops worldwide. Archbishop Charles Longley responded with a personal invitation to his home at Lambeth Palace in London, to what would be the first of many such "Lambeth Conferences."

Longley was clear from the start about what that first gathering would and would not be. In a statement on September 24, 1867, Longley noted that it had "never been contemplated that we should assume the functions of a general synod of all the Churches in full communion with the Church of England." This was not to be a legislative group, not a central authority, not a magisterium. As Longley put it, "We merely propose to discuss matters of practical interest, and pronounce what we deem expedient in resolutions which may serve as safe guides to future action."[4] Not all bishops were keen on the idea of such a gathering. The archbishop of York, the other primate in England, actually boycotted the first conference, and he was not alone. However, for the many bishops who did attend, they found it to be a wonderful opportunity for fellowship, deliberations, and common prayer and study.

What could have been a one-off event became a tradition, as Longley's successor, Archbishop Tait, called for a second Lambeth Conference a decade later. Again noting that there was "no intention whatever on the part of anybody" to make the gathering a doctrinal or disciplinary synod, Tait instead promoted it was an opportunity for "a work of love . . . that we may by friendly intercourse be able to strengthen one another's hands."[5] His successor in turn, Archbishop Benson, spoke of the "embracingness" of the Communion, calling on bishops who came to the third Lambeth Conference to affirm their "their liberty in things doubtful or indifferent."[6] The resolutions the bishops did endorse in those earliest and subsequent gatherings had to do with relations between the various member churches as well as with other Christian groups, along with issues of theological education and training, and other areas of common concern.

Additional question: Why is face-to-face gathering so important for Christians?

What is the significance of the Lambeth Conference today?

"To a world that craves for fellowship we present our message. The secret of life is fellowship."[7] These words come from the final letter of the Lambeth Conference of 1920, written soon after the tragic events of the War to End All Wars. Just one year earlier, a conference of political leaders meeting in Paris spoke of the promise of the gift of world peace, but it was a gift wrapped in retribution for past hurts. True fellowship, the bishops meeting at Lambeth proclaimed, is only possible by God's grace. To model that, they committed themselves to

---

4. The Lambeth Conferences, 1867-1948 (London: SPCK 1948), 9.

5. Ibid., 10.

6. Ibid.

7. Ibid., The Encyclical Letter for the Lambeth Conference 1920.

a new kind of communion, one achieved "not by reducing the different groups of Christians to uniformity, but by rightly using their diversity." It was a manifesto for ecumenism and a remarkable challenge to the prevailing spirit of the day.

The lessons of those earlier Lambeth Conferences have at times been forgotten in the midst of the various internal conflicts that the Communion itself has faced in subsequent decades. Yet in 2008, bishops were reminded once more that they were called to communion with one another, not necessarily agreement in all things. That conference would be noteworthy for its lack of resolutions, as participants instead gathered daily for prayer and Bible study and for what is known as "indaba," an African word that speaks of deep listening to one another, honoring the cultural and ecclesiastical differences between the various churches. As with the first Lambeth Conference, there were some who boycotted this gathering, but for the many who came, there was a renewed hope of fellowship with one another, and therefore a renewed hope of sharing the gospel of reconciliation in Christ with the world.

There will always be cynics, even in the church, and there will always be saboteurs, even within the church. But the Lambeth Conference of 2008, like the one in 1867 or the one in 1920, reminded both participants and onlookers alike that Anglican Christianity at its best has a message of peace and redemption for the world, grounded not in uniformity but in a far deeper and more profound unity that enables us to look into the eyes of the other . . . and see Christ.

Additional question: When have you seen or experienced real unity in diversity?

What is a primate? Why is ours called a presiding bishop, not an archbishop?

The primate is the chief shepherd of any one of the thirty-eight provinces that comprise the Anglican Communion. In most, but certainly not all, parts of the Communion this person is called an archbishop. Since 1978, the Anglican primates have met regularly, usually annually, at the invitation of the archbishop of Canterbury, who is *primus inter pares* or first among equals. This Primates Meeting is considered to be one of the Instruments of Unity, at which the primates engage in fellowship, prayer, Bible study, and discussion about various issues that concern them and the Communion at large. Often, at the conclusion of such gatherings, the primates issue a pastoral letter to the entire Communion which, though not binding in its authority, carries the weight of their shared influence.

From the start, the leadership of the nascent Episcopal Church chose not to have an archbishop, most likely because of concerns similar to those they had regarding not having a king, but rather a president. Thus, we have a presiding bishop. (A similar case can be found in the Scottish Episcopal Church, which has a primus instead of an archbishop.) For many years, our presiding bishop was simply the bishop with seniority, who presided over meetings of the House of Bishops. In the early twentieth century, the tradition changed as the Church gained a more corporate structure, so that henceforth the House of Bishops would elect one of their own, the election then confirmed by the House of Deputies. That new presiding bishop would relinquish the connection to and authority over a particular diocese, and focus all energies on the larger Church.

The Constitution and Canons of the Episcopal Church clearly lay out the responsibilities of the presiding bishop, who is to lead in the development of policy and strategy in the Church, speak as the representative of the Church and its episcopate, provide for an interim in a diocese without a bishop, take order for the consecration of new bishops, convene the House of Bishops, preside over meetings of the House and the General Convention when the two sessions are assembled together, and visit every diocese of the Church. The Most Rev. Katharine Jefferts Schori, the XXVI presiding bishop, is the first woman to hold that office.

Additional question: Why is it helpful for all of us for primates to meet together?

How do Episcopalians connect globally with other Anglicans?

In recent years, much discussion has taken place on what is called the Anglican Covenant, a four-part confessional statement which, when approved and signed by the various provinces that make up the Communion, would have served as a tangible point of unity. While some did approve the Covenant, others said no to it, and still others put off a vote in order to study and converse on it more. However, through the process, hard but important conversations took place within and between member churches that helped to clarify the different ways in which they try to be faithful to Christ and the mission of Christ's followers.

The Anglican Communion office has helped promote further conversations through programs such as Continuing Indaba, which continues the listening process initiated at the Lambeth Conference of 2008, and the Bible in the Life of the Church project, which explores how different provinces read and interpret the Scriptures.

The most important way in which Episcopalians build and maintain connections with other Anglicans is through companion relationships with congregations and dioceses in other parts of the Communion. Through such partnerships, there is the opportunity for mutual learning and growth, as representatives visit back and forth, gaining appreciation of the very different contexts of mission and ministry in which we find ourselves. There are also practical possibilities, as funds, expertise, programs, and human resources can be shared and allow projects to be undertaken that would never have come to fruition without such partnership. Recent years have witnessed the rise of three-way companion relationships—one example being a diocese in the Episcopal Church linked with one in the Church of England and one in the Anglican Church of Tanzania—thereby encouraging even greater possibilities of learning and shared mission.

In these and many other ways, we Episcopalians can be reminded that we are part of a larger whole, the Anglican Communion, and through this come to appreciate even more what it means to be part of the communion of saints across time and throughout the world.

Additional question: What can we learn from Christians in other parts of the world?

Are conservative Christians still welcome in the Episcopal Church?

The answer is quite definitely yes. The Episcopal Church has congregations throughout the country. Some are liberal (tend to be progressive on social and religious questions) and some are conservative (tend to be conservative on social and religious questions). However, both sides share a love for the liturgy and thoughtfulness of the Episcopal Church.

Critics of the Episcopal Church love to try and characterize the Church as too progressive. It is true that the Episcopal Church is sensitive to the ways in which we were perhaps behind the curve over the civil rights controversy of the fifties and sixties. We have as a tradition sought to repent of our inability to move more quickly in recognition of the struggle for equality our African-American brothers and sisters were involved in. It is also true that, perhaps because of this history, many in the Church are proud of our commitment to recognize the important role for women in the Church and our affirmation of our gay and lesbian brothers and sisters.

However, the Episcopal Church is bound in so many ways to love tradition. We have a Book of Common Prayer that includes material that goes back centuries. We love the Bible and allow it to figure prominently in our liturgy and worship. The overwhelming majority of bishops and clergy are committed to the key themes of the Christian drama—the Trinity and Incarnation. We share with our conservative brothers and sisters the importance of Scripture, tradition, and, in particular, the creeds.

We also welcome all perspectives. The work of discerning "what is of God" is hard. We need the range of perspectives. We appreciate the wisdom of those who push the question: What is the biblical basis of this or that innovation? We appreciate the insight of those who push the question: How can we further the work of justice in today's society?

Naturally, this can look messy at times. If you look at the church in Corinth and read behind Paul's letters to that congregation, then you will see messy is the norm. And messy can be good. We would rather all stay together in conversation than keep aspiring for a purity where other voices are excluded.

Additional question: Why do you think it is important for us to try and be in conversation with each other?

And Finally . . .

What is the future of the Episcopal Church?

One widespread myth circulating about the Episcopal Church is that it is in terminal decline. For some sociologists of religion, it looks like the historic major Protestant denominations (known as the mainline) are in trouble and have been since the 1960s. The late Richard John Neuhaus (a Roman Catholic priest who was a Lutheran pastor) was fond of saying, "The mainline, now old-line, increasingly sideline, churches of America."[1]

The truth is much more complicated. It is true that we are a small denomination. Depending on how you count the Episcopal Church, we make up less than 1 percent of the population of the United States. It is also true that since the mid-1960s, our membership has been in decline. However, membership is a very fluid indicator. A better symbol of participation is the actual attendance numbers.

We have kept attendance numbers since 1991. From 1991 to 2001, the Average Sunday Attendance (ASA) of the Episcopal Church actually grew by 18,000 or so. Now this is pretty negligible, but considering that our sister mainline denominations were really struggling through the 1990s, this is encouraging. The first decade of the twenty-first century has been difficult for the Episcopal Church. However, there are plenty of signs that this season of schism is coming to an end. In the early part of the decade, the Episcopal Church was leading the way on this cultural issue. Now midway through the second decade, mainstream culture is catching up. It was Brian

---

1. Richard John Neuhaus, "Reflections on the Institute on Religion and Democracy," October 2005, *http://theird.org/about/our-history/reflections-on-ird/*.

McClaren, the emergent church "guru," who has suggested that this can and should be the Episcopal Church moment. Here we are promising a beautiful mixture of the traditional (gorgeous prayers from different Christian traditions) with the thoughtful (a faith where you are allowed to think).

There is no reason at all why the Episcopal Church cannot recover the momentum of the nineties decade. The truth is that we are extremely robust and here to stay.

Additional question: What are the features of Episcopal worship that continues to attract a significant following?

Additional Reading

DeSilva, David, *Sacramental Life: Spiritual Formation through the Book of Common Prayer* (Downers Grove, IL: IVP Books, 2008). This book focuses on baptism, eucharist, marriage, and burial. It offers a new way to think through the important moments in life.

Higton, Mike, *Difficult Gospel: The Theology of Rowan Williams* (New York: Church Publishing, 2004). Rowan Williams is probably the most thoughtful theological mind working in Anglicanism today. This is a gentle, delightful introduction to his theology.

Markham, Ian S., *Liturgical Life Principles: How Episcopal Worship Can Lead to Healthy and Authentic Living* (New York: Morehouse Publishing, 2009). A journey through the liturgy of the Episcopal Church. The purpose is to help the liturgy connect with life.

Markham, Ian S, *Understanding Christian Doctrine* (Oxford: Wiley Blackwell, 2008). This is intended as an accessible introduction to the major themes of the Christian faith—the nature of God, reasons for belief, the Trinity, the Incarnation, Atonement, and life after death.

Prichard, Robert A, *History of the Episcopal Church* (Harrisburg, PA: Morehouse Publishing, 1999). Rightly considered a classic. Fair, balanced, and informative. A history of the Episcopal Church that is used in many Episcopal Church history courses.

Robertson, C. K., *The Book of Common Prayer: A Spiritual Treasure Chest* (Woodstock, VT: SkyLight Paths, 2013). A resource for seekers, newcomers, and longtime Episcopalians alike. A collection of passages from the Prayer Book with explanatory notes to guide readers in their own spiritual journey.

Robertson, C. K., *A Dangerous Dozen: 12 Christians Who Threatened the Status Quo* (Woodstock, VT: SkyLight Paths, 2011). With a preface by Archbishop Desmond Tutu, a compendium of tales about Christians who have challenged both societal and ecclesiastical powers, but have shown us the way to trust in and live like Jesus.

Webber, Christopher, *Welcome to the Episcopal Church: An Introduction to Its History, Faith, and Worship* (Harrisburg, PA: Morehouse Publishing, 1999). This is an accurate and delightfully brief survey of the history and life of the Episcopal Church.

Wells, Samuel, *Be Not Afraid: Facing Fear with Faith* (Grand Rapids, MI: Brazos Press, 2011). A delightful introduction to the spirit of Anglicanism. A fabulous book.

Wells, Samuel, *What Episcopalians Believe: An Introduction* (Harrisburg, PA: Morehouse Publishing, 2011). An excellent and accessible journey through the main beliefs of the Episcopal Church.